# Vietnam
## From National Liberation to 21st Century Socialism

Published by
Committees of Correspondence
Education Fund, Inc.
220 E. 42nd St, (Room 407)
New York, NY 10017
(212) 868-3773

Email: national@cc-ds.org
Web: www.cc-ds.org

**Editors: Duncan McFarland,
Paul Krehbiel and Harry Targ**

**Production and design:
Carl Davidson and Alynne Romo
Copy Editor: Ted Reich**

Cover graphic:
Grow More Cotton to Produce More Cloth
Artist:  Trong An
Central Fine Arts Company, 1982
Reprinted with permission from
The Vietnamese Women's Museum
Vietnam Women's Union

Back cover: Worker Solidarity Poster
by Paul Krehbiel, *New Age* newspaper,
October 1970

ISBN: 978-1-304-20457-8

Changmaker Publications
http://lulu.com/changemaker

# Table of Contents

Introduction. Page 1.

Chapter 1. A Nation at Work. By Paul Krehbiel. Page 5.

Chapter 2. The Vietnam Women's Union: An Effective Mass Organization. By Harry Targ. Page 25.

Chapter 3. Agent Orange: The Unmet Responsibility of the United States. By Merle Ratner. Page 28.

Chapter 4. Vietnam: 65 Years of the Struggle for National Independence and Socialism. By Tran Dac Loi. Page 32.

Chapter 5. Vietnam Update 2013: Opportunities and Challenges. By Merle Ratner and Ngo Thanh Nhan. Page 51.

Chapter 6. Origins of Doi Moi Policy in Vietnam and the Relationship to Lenin's New Economic Policy. By Duncan McFarland. Page 55.

Chapter 7. United States Foreign Policy and the Vietnam War. By Harry Targ. Page 61.

Chapter 8. What you can do to build solidarity and friendship with Vietnam. The Editors. Page 86.

# Introduction

## *By the CCDS Vietnam Committee*

For the past twenty-five years, Vietnam's economy has been one of the fastest growing in the world. With nearly full employment, it has made among the greatest improvements in living standards for its people, as well as eradicating poverty and hunger, of any country anywhere.

Vietnam is also a leader in increasing life expectancy, advancing education, and promoting the general welfare of its people. It ranks high in electing women and minority groups to decision-making bodies, and improving the quality of life for everyone. These are some of the building blocks in creating a socialist society.

How did Vietnam make these remarkable achievements, especially after many decades of war and foreign occupation?

The Committees of Correspondence for Democracy and Socialism (CCDS) sponsored socialism study delegations to Vietnam in 2009 and 2011 to find answers to these and many other questions. Our host organization was the Vietnam Women's Union, an impressive mass organization with 13 million members that made considerable efforts to show us today's Vietnam.

Most of the participants in the study tours were antiwar activists or veterans during the 1960s and 1970s. The motivation to visit Vietnam came from the passion to learn more about Vietnam today, and to demonstrate continued solidarity with people who stood for independence and against United States imperialism. In addition, many came because the war in Vietnam shaped their political consciousness. Everyone was eager to see a country that said it was building a new socialist-oriented society based on cooperation and caring, rather than the dog-eat-dog competition of Western capitalism. We saw the gains achieved under the Vietnamese "Doi Moi" (renewal) strategy of market socialism - combining elements of capitalism and socialism, and believe there are profound lessons for those of us deeply interested in creating a better world.

*New Construction in Vietnam today*

## Factories, Schools and Rebirth

The site visits included a textile factory exporting products to the US and other countries, a hospital with an Agent Orange victims ward and Da Nang University where we had discussions with students and faculty. We also visited a national minority district in the northern mountains, a Women's Union social club in the countryside, meetings with National Liberation Front veterans of the American (Vietnam) War and participated in informative presentations and probing discussions.

Cultural and educational visits included the Women's Union Museum, the national art gallery, the Ho Chi Minh Museum, the War (Crimes) Remnants Museum, as well as a Hanoi puppet show for children, and several public parks. We walked freely in commercial and residential areas and spoke with people on the street. While the tours concentrated mostly in the urban districts, group members felt they saw a lot of today's Vietnam in the short time we were there.

The delegations found a remarkable story of rebirth of an entire nation after the vast destruction of nearly 30 years of the French and American Wars. Vietnam today is a vibrant, colorful and youthful nation which has achieved remarkable economic and social progress. It has been cited by the United Nations for its accomplishments in poverty reduction, advancements in education, women's rights and in other important areas.

Vietnam is facing continuing problems as well as new and difficult ones. But, it is discussing these problems at all levels of society, in the media and on the street, including with us. Leaders of Vietnam's Communist Party and government openly discuss the obstacles, weaknesses, and mistakes they've made, including corruption and efforts to combat it, and the contradictions that capitalism and socialism have brought while existing side-by-side. The country's leaders have put forward a thoughtful and comprehensive program, both for the short and long-term, to correct the problems and improve people's lives. Vietnam says it is a socialist-oriented country working to build the foundation to create a fully socialist society where increasingly the harmful contradictions will be lessened and resolved. Our main impression was of a people and country that are confident they will succeed.

Vietnam, so prominent in US news and politics for the entire decade of 1965-75, virtually dropped out of the news as soon as the war was over. For the American policy makers, the desire was to erase the bad memory of their defeat in Vietnam and the so-called "Vietnam Syndrome" of losing a war, in order to start new imperialist wars.

## Building Friendship

This book opens a window to Vietnam, allowing us to meet a warm and hard-working people today and learn about their recent past. One of our goals is to show the efforts of the Vietnamese people as they work to transition to socialism in a global political economy dominated by capitalism.

Participants of the two delegations to Vietnam felt a responsibility to work with our fellow citizens to insist that the United States honor treaty obligations to assist with as-yet unfulfilled commitments to reconstruct the country which we bombed for over a decade. In addition, the ongoing horrific damage of Agent Orange has been barely addressed in our country, except by US Vietnam veterans, many of whom also suffer from its effects. It is our responsibility to hold the US government and chemical corporations accountable for their terrible actions. This book is also intended to preserve a basic outline history of the war in Vietnam that is more objective and truthful than what is presented in mainstream American textbooks, movies, news, and other media.

As the world's economic center shifts to Asia, Vietnam is becoming again more prominent in global affairs, especially with its important strategic position in Southeast Asia. Vietnam is today the second largest exporter of rice in the world. It also expresses solidarity with other countries, and is the principal rice supplier to Cuba, as one example.

Vietnam is a story that inspires hope for its amazing persistence in the face of colossal obstacles in retaining its independence and building a better life for its people. Vietnam is also a dynamic socialist-oriented country with profound lessons in socialist construction in the real-world conditions of late 20th century and early 21st century world capitalism.

Finally, CCDS hopes this book will encourage the growth of ties and exchanges between the American and Vietnamese people and our governments to build a growing friendship.

# Chapter 1: A Nation at Work

### *By Paul Krehbiel*

One of my first impressions upon arriving in Vietnam in March 2011 was of a people and country bustling with activity. Signs of the massive destruction from the war of 40 years earlier were largely gone from public view. Yet, behind the lush green fields and forests, historic sites, and modern building projects, were remnants of the war years.

But today, Vietnam is looking to the future, with hope and optimism. People were constructing homes and businesses, working in factories, in fields, schools, hospitals, at countless markets, producing goods in the front yards of their houses, and selling all sorts of products in stores and on the streets. We saw brand new modern buildings going up amidst old buildings from the French colonial era.

It rained most of the time we were there, but that didn't slow down this busy nation of nearly 90 million people. What is especially remarkable is that Vietnam, a country not too long ago plagued by hunger and starvation, has today one of the fastest growing economies and rising living standards in the world.  All of this has happened while much of the rest of the world economy is in the doldrums, and living standards for millions of people in many other countries are falling. What did the socialist leaders of Vietnam do to reverse this trend in their country? That and other questions were on my mind when I became part of an eight-person CCDS Study Tour of Vietnam, from March 13-27, 2011.

Our host was the 13 million member Vietnam Women's Union, one of the most influential organizations in Vietnam. Our Vietnamese guides and translators were from Peace Tours. All of our Vietnamese hosts were extremely helpful.

During our two-week stay, we met with factory workers and factory owners, students and teachers, women's groups, members of ethnic minorities, union members, artists, healthcare workers, war veterans, a leader of the Vietnam Friendship Union who is also a political leader, and others. We began in Hanoi, the nation's capital of over 6 million people. We visited the H'mong minority people in the rural area of Sapa in the northwest, visited Hue and DaNang in central Vietnam, and Ho Chi Minh City (formerly Saigon) in the south, home to over 8 million people. We also saw a small portion of the nearby tunnels of Cu Chi, 200 miles of secret underground passageways and living quarters around Saigon built by the liberation movement and which played a dramatic role in the country's ultimate achievement of independence.

## Young People

On our first day in Vietnam we walked to a nearby public square and open-air market at mid-day near Hanoi's Old Town district that stretched for many blocks which we found packed with vendors and huge crowds. The vendors, mostly young people, were selling everything from fruit, vegetables, meat and flowers, to radios and cell phones and other electronics, to shirts, pants, dresses and fabric, to chairs, tables, and other furniture, to paintings, CDs and DVDs, much of it produced in Vietnam.

We went back to the market that evening and it was still crowded. Young people stood in small groups, talking and laughing. Restau-

*Busy nightlife for young people*

rants and clubs were filled, again mostly with young people, and music spilled onto the streets. We saw very few police officers, and women of all ages walked along the streets alone or with other women even late at night, appearing to feel quite safe.

Vietnam is a nation of youth. An estimated 3 million Vietnamese were killed during the war with the Americans, which ended in 1975. The country was in ruins. But, the economy began to improve by the late 1980s, and Vietnam experienced a baby boom. Approximately 25 million people, about a third of the population, were between the ages of 15 and 29 in 2011. The median age was 27.8 years. We met Vietnamese young people working in responsible jobs in many sectors of the economy. People of all ages were warm and friendly toward us.

Since nearly everyone is working and the economy is expanding - at 7%-8% per year before the world-recession in 2008, and unemployment just 2-4%, most people have money to spend. A major purchase is a motor-bike. The streets were crammed with them, replacing bicycles as the main means of getting around. In some places, there were few stop signs or traffic lights, so motorists zigged zagged past each other and pedestrians like seasoned veterans. I never saw an accident, though it seemed like there should have been many.

We visited the President Ho Chi Minh Mausoleum in Hanoi. Despite the rain, thousands of people stood patiently in line for hours to view the preserved body of the founding president of modern day Vietnam.

Ho Chi Minh is revered here as the father of Vietnam. We toured a museum next to the mausoleum that is dedicated to his life and work where we met large groups of school children and their teachers.

Everyone in our CCDS group brought small gifts to give to Vietnamese that we met, and I gave a drawing I did of Ho Chi Minh during the war years to the directors of the Ho Chi Minh Museum.

Large billboards are located around the city and countryside commemorating or promoting important events and several featured photos of Ho Chi Minh and messages he gave to the people. This billboard commemorates the 65th anniversary of the August 1945 Revolution when Vietnam established its independence.)

Vietnam is a spectacularly beautiful country. We visited Sapa, in northwest Vietnam not far from China, where low-lying streams of fog curled around the waists of rugged mountains and meandered into softly rolling river valleys.

## H'mong Ethnic Minority Group

There we met people from the local ethnic minority group, the H'mong. When our tour bus pulled into the small town of Sapa, we were greeted by four smiling young women who were selling locally hand-crafted scarves and other products. They seemed genuinely happy to meet us. Their native clothing

was decorated with brightly-colored stitching and beads. Their English was excellent, learned from the English-language classes they took in school and from talking to English-speaking tourists.

We asked each other similar questions, and they eagerly responded. "How old are you? Are you married? Do you have children? What did you study in school? What kind of work do you do? What is life like where you live?"

As we walked together through their village talking, our group saw their small wooden homes dotting the hillsides. Men were tending fields, cattle and young children. Women were making products for sale and older children were helping or playing.

This was a poor, but vibrant community. While Vietnam has reduced poverty from 58% in 1993, to under 12% in 2009, pockets of poverty still exist in some remote rural areas like Sapa. Since this is a poor area inhabited by an ethnic minority group, the government has taken special measures to offer economic loans and other assistance.

The city of Sapa has a small but growing tourist industry, bringing jobs and money into the area.In our short time together, we saw that the H'mong have the same hopes and dreams of all people: to improve their lives, care for their children and live together in a harmonious community.

*Sapa's 'Holiday Inn'*

We left the village and walked through a stunning mountain valley to visit a primary and secondary school to visit a classroom of young girls and boys. They study the Vietnamese language, history, and culture, reading, writing, math, science, English, vocational classes, about the life of Ho Chi Minh, and the struggle for national independence. While in northern Vietnam we also travelled down a beautiful river framed by Vietnam's unique sculpted mountains, riding in traditional Vietnamese boats.

We also visited the fa-
mous Temple of Liter-
ature in Hanoi, where
reading, writing, and
the study of history
and culture has flour-
ished for centuries.

## Art, Culture and Education

In central Vietnam,
we visited Hoi An, a
beautifully preserved
port city dating back
to the 15th century.
It is recognized as a
World Heritage site
by the United Nations Educational, Scientific, and Cultural Organization (UNESCO).

Hoi An's beautiful boats, tree-line streets, classic Southeast Asian architec-
ture, flower gardens, Pagodas and Buddhist temples, art and clothing shops,
and open-air cafes make this a favorite location for locals and tourists.

Art and culture are an
important part of Viet-
namese life. While in Hue
in central Vietnam, we
attended a performance
at a former royal theater
that celebrated the long
and rich culture of the
Vietnamese people. Per-
formers dressed in tra-
ditional costumes and
played soft lilting traditional Vietnamese music.

*Two students at Da Nang University*

We visited a large artists' workshop and watched skilled sculptors create
animals and people out of marble, quartz and other minerals. We also
visited several art galleries in various parts of the country. Education is

a high priority for the Vietnamese and the government has worked hard to provide schooling for all children and young people. We visited professors and students at DaNang University. The students politely answered our questions about the war, but said they were focused on building Vietnam today.  They were born well after the end of the war, they reminded us.  One engineering student told us that he was proud of his country and his parents and the struggle to achieve independence. But, he and his friends said they wanted "Vietnam to be known also as a modern and progressive industrial country." Several said they wanted to transfer to top universities in the United States to get the training they would need to take important jobs in industry and public affairs, and then return home to help build their country.  Many Vietnamese are already doing that. Many of the most socially-minded work in large public organizations.One of the largest is the Vietnam Women's Union, our gracious hosts.

## Women

We visited the national office of the Vietnam Women's Union (VWU) in Hanoi, toured their excellent Women's Museum, and met with several of its leaders and staff.  One of its leaders travelled with our group for a significant portion of our tour, and along with the staff, did everything possible to make our trip enjoyable, educational, and memorable.

*Women's Union greets us.*

The VWU has 14,472 local chapters in every city, town, village and rural area in Vietnam, allowing the organization to address the needs of women and girls in every part of the country. Its goals today are to assist in the education and training of girls and women, improve their material and spiritual lives, advance their rights, nurture happy families, and to "cultivate Vietnamese women who are patriotic, knowledgeable, healthy, skillful, dynamic, innovative, cultured, and kind-hearted."

All are important goals. I took special note of the words "kind-hearted." Few organizations that I know of list this as one of its goals. But, what an excellent goal, I thought. And being kind-hearted isn't reserved just for women. Men are expected to be kind-hearted too.

We visited several projects initiated, run, or assisted by the Vietnam Women's Union. One was a small garment shop called Thien Tam, located in DaNang, where the US had a big military base and people suffered greatly from the war.

Thien Tam is a special workshop. It was founded by a woman who had been exposed to Agent Orange during the war. She wanted to establish a garment shop to employ others who had also been exposed. She met with the VWU and received financial and organizational assistance. We saw workers at sewing machines making a variety of garments. Since they have special needs, they do not have to "compete" in the market place. But, they make a contribution to the economy by producing useful products, and they receive a paycheck that helps them survive.

*Paul Krehbiel (left) and Duncan McFarland (center) speak with workers at the Thien Tam textile workshop with help of Vietnamese interpreter (standing).*

## Agent Orange

Agent Orange is a very toxic herbicide that was sprayed by the US military during the war to defoliate forests, jungle and crop-lands, and it became a brutal weapon of war against humans as well. Over

20 million gallons of the dioxin-laced poison were sprayed over most of South Vietnam, an area the size of Massachusetts.

Some 5 million Vietnamese were exposed to Agent Orange, 400,000 people died from it and 500,000 or more suffered illnesses such as cancer and birth defects in three generations of children. Many or most of the 2 million American servicemen and women who were sent to Vietnam are presumed to have been exposed to Agent Orange as well, and many have died or are ill from it. Monsanto, and Dow Chemical, the maker of napalm, were the manufacturers of Agent Orange.

Several of the older workers at Thien Tam told us that after the war, with the economy in ruins, their disabilities made it difficult to get a job. They were homeless, lived on the street begging for food, and were ill and malnourished. One worker told us through an interpreter, "If it hadn't been for this shop, I don't know what would have happened to me. I might not be alive today."

The Vietnam Women's Union also establishes social centers for women all over the country. We visited one at Quang Thanh - Quang Dien, in a rural area outside Hue, another region that suffered heavily from the war. This center was created to help single women of all ages who were struggling with financial, family or personal problems. Some had lost husbands in the war, some from divorce, some never married, and some left an abusive husband. The center provides a safe

place for women, job training and social skills, and a place where women can socialize and make friends.

When we arrived at the center, a meeting of about 50 women was underway. The women took a break so we could introduce ourselves and ask questions of each other. Towards the end of the session, the women played a word game that had everyone laughing.

We also visited Peace House, a shelter for women victimized by sexual trafficking. Laws prohibit exploiting women for sex in Vietnam, but some young Vietnamese girls are lured into the sex trade by promises of careers in modeling and acting. This often is done by traffickers from other nearby countries that take the young women out of Vietnam, hold them as captives and force them to work in the sex industry. When girls escape or are freed, some come to the Peace House for care, counseling, and rehabilitation. When their psychological condition improves, they enroll in training programs for legitimate jobs and careers. We met women who worked at the Peace House and saw some of the art work that patients did there to help them deal with their trauma and recovery.

This shelter also helps women who have been victims of domestic violence. There is a child care center at Peace House, so mothers can rehabilitate while their children are cared for. Another project of the Vietnam Women's Union is the Center for Women and Development (CWD). The CWD deals with many women's issues including domestic abuse. As women gain more rights and improve their lives, some men felt threatened. One result has been domestic abuse. The CWD's mission is to help women who are victims of "beating, sexual violence or scolding." It is noteworthy that "scolding" or verbal abuse is seen as a form of abuse. Scolding is generally defined as criticizing or reprimanding harshly, often involving anger, and it connotes berating or putting one down.

The CDW wants to eliminate scolding from society. The slogan of the CWD is: "We are Always Beside You." It was clear everywhere we went that the welfare of everyone was important in Vietnam. While individuals were encouraged to become all they were capable of becoming, individual achievements should be accomplished in a way that respects and advances the common good. This message is conveyed to the entire society by government leaders, the mass media, culture and other important organizations and institutions. It is a cornerstone in building a humane and caring socialist society.

We saw examples of kindness and politeness everywhere we went. People talked to each other in a friendly, respectful way. This kindness, however, shouldn't be interpreted as weakness. The Vietnamese, both women and men, have a long history of fighting fiercely for their independence, respect, and against injustice. While in Hue, we also visited and had lunch at a Pagoda with Buddhist monks and learned more about the role Buddhists played in resisting the repressive US-imposed Diem government on the people of South Vietnam. We saw religious temples in every area we visited.

During the war, the American people heard repeatedly from our government and the mass media that there was no religious or intellectual freedom in communist North Vietnam. We don't know what life was like then, and got only a glimpse if it in March of 2011. But, in addition to meeting with Buddhists in their Temple, we spoke with Vietnamese who freely talked about good things and problems in Vietnam, and ideas about how to correct the problems.

In one large modern bookstore we visited on a major street, which was very crowded, we saw books expressing a broad range of political ideas, from the right-wing capitalism of Ronald Reagan to the democratic ideas of John Locke and Thomas Jefferson, to the national liberation and socialist ideas of the Communist leader Ho Chi Minh.

## Tu Du Hospital

We travelled to Ho Chi Minh City and visited Tu Du Obstetric Hospital, a leading women's and children's hospital. Our group was invited into a warmly decorated meeting room where we met with

10 hospital staff, including administrators, doctors, nurses and other workers.

Tu Du hospital is responsible for overseeing family health care in the area from DaNang to the Mekong Delta. The hospital employs a staff of nearly 2,000, of whom 85% are women. All of the doctors except one are women. Tu Du is a comprehensive hospital for the residents of Ho Chi Minh City, the staff also does massive public health outreach in the southern half of Vietnam.

One big campaign is providing midwife training for women in remote areas and the dissemination of birthing kits through a partnership with The Birthing Kit Foundation of Australia. The Foundation wrote that world-wide, "every 90 seconds a women dies of complications related to pregnancy and childbirth," primarily due to infections from unclean birthing sites. This hospital brings sanitary birthing products and training to thousands of midwives and expecting women, saving thousands of lives every year.

*Melodi Shapiro, a Registered Nurse with CCDS group, at Tu Do Hospital*

Another program at Tu Du Hospital that sets it apart from most other hospitals anywhere in the world is that it is also a major hospital for the treatment and care of children born sick and disabled from Agent Orange poisoning. We visited this area of the hospital, called Peace Village. We saw third generation children who were severely disabled and deformed from Agent Orange poisoning who were lovingly cared for by the medical staff at Peace Village. Agent Orange got into food, water, and humans, and has been passed on to three generations of Vietnamese.

There is a campaign in the United States to get our government, and Dow Chemical, and Monsanto to make reparations to the Vietnamese and US servicemen and women who were affected by Agent Orange. Learn more about how you can help this campaign by reading Merle Ratner's article later in this book.

## Textile Workers

We also visited several other workplaces. One was a privately- owned Vietnamese textile mill of about 700 workers in Ho Chi Minh City where various types of threads were spun. We toured the factory for about a half an hour with our hosts from the Women's Union and translators from Peace Tours, and spoke to workers everywhere we went.

The factory was quite clean. There was no lint or dust in the air. The machinery looked to be fairly modern and efficient. We saw no break- downs or downtime. There was some noise, but you could talk easily to a group of people near you without yelling, while standing near a

machine that was running. Everyone we spoke with said their lives had improved since working in the factory. They are earning more money and a number have made good friends with co-workers.

After the tour, we met with the owner and several managers and union leaders. The owner said that he established his company in 1990 under the new government policy that encouraged new busi- ness development. He said that with the help of the government they are working to produce products for export that will help bring more money into the country to help raise the standard of living. His com- pany produces 5,000 tons of material a year and exports primarily to the United Arab Emirates, Germany, Spain, and the US. The work- ers are members of a Vietnamese union, and their union's Executive

Board meets with management every 3 months to discuss workers' problems in the factory, programs to expand workers' skills, and production.

The majority of the members of our delegation were union members, so we asked a number of questions about the union and workers rights. The workers have a Collective Bargaining Agreement (CBA) with management that spells out workers' conditions of work. There are labor laws in effect as well. If the company violates the CBA or labor law, workers can bring these grievances to the company or appropriate government agency, just as unionized workers do in the United States. If a violation has taken place, an order will be given to correct it.

The union leader told us he had been a factory worker, and now was the president of the local union. He said there was a Communist Party organization in this factory which is still small but active. We saw a Communist Party dues collection box with a red hammer and sickle on it in the room where we met and photos of Marx and Engels on the walls.

Vietnamese workers have the legal right to strike and there are numerous strikes, mostly at foreign-owned factories where the pace of work is faster and working conditions harsher. These strikes are often wildcat strikes, and union officials and sometimes government representatives get involved in resolving the dispute by trying to negotiate some redress of the workers complaints. This has led to anger by some factory owners. Strikes are rare at state-owned companies, where workers are treated better.

## Five Types of Business

There are five general types of businesses in Vietnam: small individual or family-owned businesses, Vietnamese-owned businesses that employ workers, foreign-owned businesses that employ workers, joint foreign-Vietnamese businesses, and state owned businesses that employ workers. While we saw workers at this textile factory working steadily, we did not see them pushed to work faster, nor did they appear to be straining or suffering while working.

Of course, this was one small glimpse of one factory so it would be impossible to make a general assessment of working conditions for Vietnamese workers as a whole. We didn't learn how often labor grievances are resolved to the satisfaction of the workers, and in con-

versations with workers in the factory, it seemed a couple of them didn't know much about the union. As a long-time union member and full-time union representative in the United States, I unfortunately have witnessed this situation in some of our unionized workplaces, despite efforts to interest and involve workers in the union.

## War Crimes

We visited the War (Crimes) Remnants Museum in Ho Chi Minh City that explained in text and photos the sordid history of American war and occupation and the Vietnamese people's resistance and ultimate victory. We saw large groups of school children there with their teachers. One section showed the world-wide opposition to the war against Vietnam, including from our own peace movement in the United States. Our group donated additional materials from the American anti-war movement to this museum. We also met with liberation fighters and learned how they resisted the US bombing and invasion of their country.

Of special interest was our visit to the Cu Chi tunnels, 200 miles of secret tunnels and living quarters underground in and around Ho Chi Minh City (formerly Saigon) that Vietnamese liberation fighters used to escape US bombing, and to launch surprise attacks on the foreign occupation army.

We went into some of the tunnels, which were built on three levels. There were kitchens, meeting and sleeping rooms, a small makeshift hospital, workshops, and offices - one still had an old typewriter on a table that was used to write letters and leaflets during  the war. We also saw small narrow tunnels and secret hatch doors that connected this vast underground network.

The Vietnamese ran long bamboo shoots from their underground stoves to the surface of the forest floor to carry cooking smoke out of their tunnels and into the forest. They cooked when there was fog in the forest so the smoke would blend in with it, and no sign of human activity could be detected by US troops on the ground in the area, or by US airplanes flying overhead.

Eventually the US military discovered a few of these underground passageways, and fierce battles were fought inside the tunnels. The Vietnamese used secret trap doors to hide the rest of the tunnel network from American "tunnel rats," as the soldiers who went into these tunnels were called. This was a hard way to fight the Vietnamese; so, the US military pulled out its troops and repeatedly bombed much of this area and sprayed it with Agent Orange to destroy the jungles and forests. When we were there, we saw bomb craters from the war, and areas defoliated by Agent Orange. In a nearby conference hall, we met with former Vietnamese liberation fighters who lived and fought in these tunnels over 40 years ago when they were very young men.

## Socialism

Earlier in our study tour, we met with Tran Dac Loi, Vice-President of the Vietnam Peace and Development Foundation. Loi candidly discussed Vietnamese society, both its successes and its weaknesses and problems. He explained that after achieving total liberation in 1975, the Vietnam Communist Party and government tried to build socialism based on putting most of the economy in the state sector. But Vietnam faced many difficulties, including a war-ravaged economy and a country plagued by poverty and starvation, inadequate productive forces and trained personnel, a US-imposed economic blockade of Vietnam, and internal weaknesses and mistakes made by Vietnam's leaders.

*Discussion on the economy*

All of this resulted in a very sluggish economy that was in crisis. The government and Communist Party changed course and implemented "doi moi," Vietnamese for "renewal." Maintaining state-owned public sector businesses in key economic areas, like banking, transportation, energy, basic manufacturing industries, and communications, they opened up other sectors of the economy and encouraged privately-owned individual and family businesses, cooperative businesses, and private local and foreign businesses. They have what they call a socialist-oriented market economy. They also negotiated an end the US economic blockade with President Clinton.

All of these changes greatly improved Vietnam's economy, and the lives of its people, while having to compete in a ruthless world capitalist economy. Loi said that the party and government see that developing a modern industrial economy is a prerequisite for building a socialist society, and a mixed economy is essential to help them accomplish that. Also, it is important to continually increase the educational and cultural level of the people, and broaden their rights.

The Vietnam Communist Party held its 11th National Congress from January 12-19, 2011 and stated that one of its goals was "to make

Vietnam by 2020 basically a modern-oriented industrial country and that by the mid-21st century a modern industrial, prosperous, strong, democratic, equitable and advanced country steadily heading toward socialism."

Clearly, Vietnam sees that building a socialist society is a process that takes time. Yet, there are obstacles. Loi said Vietnam faces a number of pressing problems today. One is corruption by a small number of individuals in both the Communist Party and in the government. Loi said there is a campaign to eradicate it. We saw efforts to highlight this problem in articles in Vietnam's English-language newspaper, Viet Nam News. A second problem is the growing disparity in wealth. A third is the growing threat of global warming/climate change, which is affecting Vietnam with rising sea levels.

A fourth problem is an ideological struggle, complicated by the relentless barrage of culture, ideas and actions from major capitalist countries, led by the US, that promotes individual competitiveness, getting ahead at the expense of others, consumerism, adoration of corporate CEOs and the very wealthy, and the glorification of war and violence - all core elements of capitalism. This ideological attack by the US and some oth-

er capitalist countries, combined with behind-the-scenes sabotage, is aimed at undermining the socialist foundation of Vietnamese society, and the Vietnamese government. Loi said that socialism isn't a foreign idea, as all societies have some socialist features, including the United States.

*Temple of Literature*

We agreed. We said we knew what he was taking about regarding the ideological war, because we face that negative cultural and ideological assault on the American people daily. It's multi-faceted and sophisticated, intended to mislead and confuse people into acting against their best interests and the best interests of the country. We all agreed that there is a constant battle to win the hearts and minds of people everywhere, either for a more humane society, or a more cut-throat one.

I realized that the war against Vietnam isn't over. It has taken different forms. It is similar to the intensified attacks made on Americans by the political right in our country in their campaign to force their brand of a more inhumane capitalism on our people. This assault has specifically targeted the working-class and unions, communities of color, women, the poor, the public sector, and any group or institution that works to protect the common good.

My trip to Vietnam 36 years after the American war ended there, made me see that the Vietnamese people and the American people are engaged in the same struggle against the same opponent. I also saw more clearly that the transition from capitalism to socialism is a long, arduous process, wrought with advances and setbacks. The goal is to create a more humane society. We do that by achieving and expanding everything that is life-affirming, and opposing everything that is life-opposing. That weakens the worst of capitalism and strengthens the best of socialism. Socialism, ultimately, is the future of humanity.

# Chapter 2: The Vietnam Women's Union: An Effective Mass Organization

## By Harry Targ

We arrived at a rural Vietnamese women's club sponsored by the Vietnam Women's Union (VWU) in Quang Thanh near Hue in time to be ushered into a meeting of 50 local single women. Discussion was animated, self-assured, and clearly engaged. Members listened to each other, respected what each had to say, and evidenced not one iota of shyness even though their discussion of women's health, environmental, and other immediate issues was being observed by eight American guests and a Vietnam Women's Union official from Hanoi.

We had already been to a briefing at the Center for Women and Development's new building, and the Women's Museum in Hanoi. We had visited Peace House, a shelter for Vietnamese women victimized by sexual trafficking, part of the CWD project to provide shelter, training, and advocacy for women victimized by domestic violence or sexual trafficking. All of these venues were part of the national activi-

ties of the Vietnam Women's Union. The VWU was clearly well organized at the center, clear of purpose and commitment and connected
to regional and local bodies of women throughout the country.

The Vietnam Women's Union, one of six major mass organizations
in the country, was founded in 1930, just before the formation of
the Indochinese Communist Party. In socialist theory and practice,
mass organizations are designed to mobilize major populations who
require and are committed to social change in their societies. While
their ideas and programs parallel those of local Communist parties,
they are committed to meeting the immediate needs of workers,
women, youth, farmers, war veterans, and others whether they are
members of political parties or not. Also, effective mass organizations require both leadership and authentic and active participation
from the grassroots.

As far as we could tell, the VWU is a model mass organization. It
has levels of activity and participation at the national and provincial
levels as well as in districts and small village communes. There are
13 million VWU members. As indicated in a VWU pamphlet: "Since its
foundation, VWU has transformed itself fully into a women's social-
political and developmental organization, which is mandated to protect women's legitimate rights and strive for gender equality."

Levels of organization of the Vietnamese Women's Union consist of a
National Congress, a Central Executive Committee, a Presidium and
provincial, district, and communal organizations. The VWU has 16
departments including communication and education, family and social affairs, international relations, ethnic and religious affairs, law
and policy, and departments overseeing museums, a newspaper,
and publishing. Our tour was organized by one of the departments,
Peace Tours.

## Empowering Women

The VWU emphasizes organizational tasks ranging from supporting
and building women's skills and autonomy at the local level to greater political influence at the national level. The commitment to goals
which were identified as critical for the recent period, 2007-2012,
were reflected in what we saw. These included raising women's consciousness, knowledge, and capacity, promoting gender equality at
all levels of society, promoting economic development, building the
VWU as a national organization, and building networks of relationships with progressive organizations around the world.

VWU short-term goals, identified in their literature seemed plausible based on our brief observation. These included targeting 70% of poor women for support " to reduce poverty and eliminate hunger," and "supporting more than 90% of female-headed poor households, with the goal of 40 to 50% escaping from poverty."

One of the VWU departments, the Center for Women and Development, concentrates particularly on giving support to victims and overcoming violence and sexual trafficking of women. Peace House, with aid from overseas Non-Governmental Organizations (NGOs), was opened in March, 2007, to construct a model shelter for abused Vietnamese women. A CWD report indicated that "The Peace House has supported women and children who suffered from domestic violence from all over the country. The numbers of women and children receiving the services of the Peace House are increasing and after leaving the Peace House they are new persons, more independent and able to protect themselves and their children."

Reflecting on guided tours such as the CCDS visit to Vietnam can have profound long-term impacts on participants, even though it is recognized that such tours are designed to show host successes while minimizing problems or organizational deficits. However, among the indisputable strengths of the VWU are the following:

1. VWU is truly a mass organization in the best sense of that term. It carries out policies representing the interests of a large percentage of women in Vietnamese society at all levels--from the rural commune to the nation.

2. A fundamental component of all VWU work is the belief that there is dignity in each member. Each Vietnamese woman has the right to fulfill her life to the full limit of societal resources and to be an active agent in that fulfillment.

3. Government, party, and mass organization, all have as their uppermost obligation to serve the people. This means that these entities continue to struggle to overcome class exploitation, gender oppression, and racial and ethnic discrimination.

Several of the tour participants, only partially in jest, wondered if progressives in the United States could hire Vietnam Women's Union organizers to help us reorder institutions and policies in the United States.

# Chapter 3. Agent Orange: The Unmet Responsibility of the United States

## By Merle Ratner

Agent Orange is an ongoing crime against humanity committed by the US government against the people of Vietnam more than 30 years ago. The terrible reality is that the Agent Orange that was sprayed over the people and land of Vietnam for many years has lodged in the bodies of those exposed and in the land, water and food chain. A third generation of Vietnamese families is now suffering from horrific birth defects.

Agent Orange is not the only legacy of the US war. During its war against Vietnam, the US government used massive amounts of firepower, dropping more than 10 million tons of bombs and other ammunition - twice the total tonnage of all bombs and ammunition dropped by all the parties in the Second World War, and equivalent to the total power of 200 atomic bombs of the type exploded in Hiroshima and Nagasaki.

Now, even 37 years after the end of the war, every day unexploded ordinance kill people in Vietnam's countryside, including many children. Other types of chemical warfare were also used, including napalm, manufactured by Dow Chemical, which continues to leave its mark on the bodies of those who were burned by its flames.

But it is Agent Orange that has had the most deadly legacy. In Vietnam, for almost a decade, from 1961 to 1971, the U.S. sprayed about 80 million liters (more than 21 million US gallons) of this chemical weapon over an area up to 25% of the territory of South Vietnam, destroying millions of acres of forest and crops. Agent Orange was used to kill plants and trees to force the people away from their land and to deprive them of the means to survive. Over 30,000 hamlets in Vietnam, with a population of almost 5 million villagers, were subject to direct sprayings. Dioxin was also sprayed in the border areas of Cambodia and Laos.

The most toxic ingredient in Agent Orange is dioxin, one of the most deadly substances known to science. Dioxin is a by-product of the manufacture of Agent Orange and could have been greatly reduced if the production process had been slowed down. But Dow and Monsanto and the other corporate criminals who produced it were so eager to rack up super profits from its sale that they continued to make "dirty" Agent Orange containing large amounts of dioxin. Documents show that both the US government and the chemical manufacturers of Agent Orange - most notably Dow Chemical and Monsanto - knew early on that its use would cause lethal consequences to those it was sprayed on.

*Agent Orange victims across generations.*

It's also no accident that the countries where the US has used toxic weapons, like Agent Orange, are overwhelmingly Third World countries. In an expression of the racism that characterized the war, Pentagon officials said publicly that Vietnamese people valued life less than American people. The US government continues to use chemical weapons in Third World countries such as Iraq and Afghanistan.

## Affecting Third Generation Children

Vietnam was ground zero for the US spraying of Agent Orange, sickening, maiming and disabling millions of people and destroying large areas of the land and environment. The human cost is found in a wide range of diseases including cancers, heart conditions, diabetes, and Parkinson's. Exposure to Agent Orange results in reproductive abnormalities including fetuses dying in-utero and stillbirths.

The dioxin in Agent Orange also remains in the land and water of Vietnam, contaminating fish and fowl. In 28 hot spots in southern and central Vietnam, people continue to be sickened by contact with the remnants of Agent Orange that the US left. Vietnam's environment and bio-diversity has been affected - something that the International People's Tribunal of Conscience in Support of the Vietnamese Victims of Agent Orange called ecocide.

## Agent Orange, American GIs and Others

The horrible effects of Agent Orange continue to affect our communities around the world. US veterans (as well as veterans of US allies like South Korea, Australia, New Zealand, Canada and Puerto Rico) suffer from a wide range of dioxin-related diseases and fought for and receive disability and health care. Vietnamese-Americans who fought in the war in their country of origin similarly suffer from cancers, heart disease, type 2 diabetes and a many other illnesses. Civilians who lived in areas in Vietnam that were sprayed and then came to the US are affected as well.

But Agent Orange does not only affect those who were directly exposed; it affects the genes, resulting in serious birth defects and illnesses in the children and grandchildren of those who were sprayed. While the children and grandchildren of victims in the US and other countries are affected by these birth defects, the impact on Vietnam is particularly acute.

In many families, three generations are sick or disabled, usually living in poverty due to the necessity of caretaking. A public health crisis is looming as many of the older generation, who were directly sprayed with Agent Orange, die early of cancers or heart conditions, leaving severely birth-defected children without anyone to take care of them.

In the US, Agent Orange affected veterans receive some benefits but their children receive none. Vietnamese-Americans and their children remain ignored and unassisted.

The US government has allocated some millions of dollars for clean-up of one of the hot spots in Vietnam and for aid to the disabled in the area (the US still refuses to recognize the human victims as affected by Agent Orange.) However, the funds are completely inadequate to address the problem the US caused and the assistance has not reached many of those who need it most.

## Relief and Responsibility Needed

The Vietnamese government gives assistance to some of the most seriously affected victims. The mass organization which represents the victims, the Vietnam Association for Victims of Agent Orange/dioxin, gives additional assistance and runs various community programs throughout the country. But Vietnam is still a poor country and does not have the resources to provide all that is needed. It is those who willfully created the problem - the US government and Dow, Monsanto and the other corporations - who must meet their responsibility to those whom they have harmed!

This is why the Vietnam Agent Orange Relief & Responsibility Campaign (VAORRC), a project of Veterans for Peace, was formed in early 2005. A coalition of Vietnamese-Americans, veterans and other peace and justice activists, the Campaign educates and organizes people in the US to achieve justice for Agent Orange sufferers. VAORRC holds educational events, hosts delegations of Agent Orange victims from Vietnam and sends delegations to Vietnam. We raise money for our partner group, the Vietnam Association for Victims of Agent Orange/dioxin, which cares for and advocates on behalf of, the victims in Vietnam. Our Campaign believes that whether in Southeast Asia or in the US, the victims of Agent Orange must have their needs addressed by those who are responsible for making them suffer. Through our Campaign's efforts, a bill is being introduced in Congress called the Victims of Agent Orange Relief Act of 2013, which aims to provide assistance to Agent Orange victims.

Together, we can meet our responsibility to truly and finally end the US war against Vietnam! We believe that the concern and political will to achieve this exists and urge readers to join us! Everyone can help. See Chapter 8, What you can do.

# Chapter 4. Vietnam: 65 Years of the Struggle for National Independence and Socialism

*By Tran Dac Loi*

## The August 1945 Revolution and the birth of a people's democratic state

In 1858, the French colonialists invaded Vietnam and step by step imposed the colonial yoke on the Vietnamese people. The rulers did not bring "civilization," "liberty" "equality" and "fraternity" to our country but instead implemented a regime designed to exploit our natural resources and human labor, based on a strengthening of the feudal system which relied on landlords to maintain political and economic control, and also enforced high taxation rates. To support their brutality, the French built more prisons than schools. Illiteracy, hunger and poverty spread across the country. Towards the end of World War II, Japanese fascists also arrived in Vietnam and collaborated with the French in ruling Vietnam. In 1945 alone, two million Vietnamese (nearly one tenth of the total population at the time) died of starvation.

Many resistance and patriotic movements took place, but all were brutally and bloodily suppressed. In the fall of 1945, these resistance movements finally succeeded under the leadership of the Vietnam Communist Party and Ho Chi Minh. This was the historic August Revolution, and on September 2, 1945, President Ho Chi Minh proclaimed the independence of Vietnam and declared the formation of the Democratic Republic of Vietnam.

This revolution changed the fate of the country and the Vietnamese people. On the one hand, independence was regained from Japanese fascists and their French collaborators, putting an end to more than 80 years of French colonialism in Vietnam. On the other hand, the revolution put an end to the feudal system which had existed for a thousand years, forming a republic and democratic system with the working people as its masters.

Vietnam's August 1945 revolution was truly a people's revolution. At that point, the Communist Party had only five thousand members all over the country. But the support and power of the people forced the Japanese army and its puppet government to surrender when the last emperor, Bao Dai, resigned, and the power was handed over to the people.

The newly formed government continued to face both external and internal enemies, with the ongoing devastating starvation and severe socio-economic situation in the country. There was no standing army and not even the financial resources to operate. Two weeks after the republic had been proclaimed, people from all over the country initiated the Gold Week to donate valuables, collect money, gold and even rice in support of the new government.

The new government declared three immediate tasks: fighting hunger, illiteracy, and foreign invaders. All existing food storages were opened to distribute rice to the people and land was given to peasants for cultivation of short-term crops to cope with the famine. President Ho Chi Minh called upon the people and set his own example of sharing his everyday ration of food with the poor.

A campaign called 'popular learning' was launched and spread nationwide. Anyone who could write or read would teach others. As there were not enough schools and classes, books, paper or pens, the teaching was done across the country in many innovative forms: in the rice fields, on the roads, at pagodas, temples, in markets, at

home, with ash, sticks, on the floor, walls, etc.  As a result, after a
short period of time, a significant part of the population was able to
read and write at a basic level.

The provisional government headed by Ho Chi Minh held free elections for the first time in our history on 6 January 1946 which gave
full legitimacy to the new government. The election was held demo-
cratically in the presence of the British, French, Japanese, and Chinese
Kuomintang troops.  Ho Chi Minh and the Vietnamese communists
gained the absolute majority of votes, and worked with other parties to form a coalition National Assembly and a Government.  The
National Assembly approved the first Constitution of the Democratic
Republic of Vietnam, affirming the independence of the nation and
the basic rights of its people.

One of the important policies adopted by the revolutionary government was "land to the tillers," a policy that changed the destiny of
the peasants who accounted for the absolute majority of the total
Vietnamese population.

Ho Chi Minh and his Government introduced policies of gender equality, national unity, and solidarity amongst religions, which received
the strong support of the people.

It could be said that, as a result of the August revolution, the Democratic Republic of Vietnam was qualitatively a new type of state - truly
of the people, for the people and by the people - which came into
being, survived and overcame numerous challenges thanks largely to
the strong support of the people. This explains the nature of today's
relationships between Vietnamese people as well as their organizations and their state.

## 30 years of resistance struggle for national independence

Despite the fact that the Democratic Republic of Vietnam was created
by the will, aspirations and strong support of the Vietnamese people
through the most democratic and freest election in the nation's history, Western powers did not wish to accept its existence. The young
republic had to face the second aggression of French colonialists
backed by the US imperialists. The uneven fight between the Vietnamese people and French army lasted nearly 9 years and was brought to
an end by the historic victory at Dien Bien Phu in 1954. The French
had to sign the Geneva Accords, and peace was restored in the North
with the internationally recognized independence of Vietnam.

According to the Geneva Accords, Vietnam was temporarily divided into two parts along the 17th parallel, and the country was expected to be reunified after two years through a general election. However, the election and reunification did not happen. The US imperialists sabotaged the Geneva Accords and replaced the French in the South. They knew that if there would be a general election, Ho Chi Minh and his government would have been supported by the absolute majority of the population. They therefore installed a puppet dictatorial government in the South in order to divide the country and repress the patriotic movements in the South and waged a war of destruction against the North.

*French troops surrendering after Dien Bien Phu*

Executing policies with names like 'kill all, burn all and destroy all' and 'bomb North Vietnam back to the stone age' the U.S. military and their allies dropped four times the tonnage of bombs used in World War II in Vietnam, which is equivalent to 725 nuclear bombs dropped in Hiroshima and Nagasaki. More than 3 million Vietnamese were killed and 4 million were wounded. At the same time, the US military used up to 80 million liters of chemicals to "clear" the land. They sprayed over 45 million liters of Agent Orange containing nearly 400 kg dioxin, the most toxic of all the chemicals discovered so far. In Vietnam, an estimated 4.8 million people have fallen victim to Agent Orange/dioxin and millions of others are carriers of deadly diseases; hundreds of thousands of children continue to be born with birth deformities. A large part of our forest was destroyed, and the infrastructure devastated. Unexploded ordinance is still spread over a large area of land and continues to pose a threat to the lives and livelihood of many people in the South of Vietnam. And today, 35 years after the end of the war, there are up to 300,000 Vietnamese still missing in their own homeland.

Yet, the brutality of the strongest imperialist power could not subjugate the will of the Vietnamese people. Under the leadership of the Communist Party and Ho Chi Minh, in the spirit that "Nothing is more precious than independence and freedom," the Vietnamese people once again rose up in a struggle for more than 20 years against the US imperialists and their puppet regime in the South. After the American forces withdrew from Vietnam as a result of the Paris Agreement of January 1973, our liberation forces intensified their offensive, culminating in the historic Ho Chi Minh Campaign, completely liberating the South, and reunifying the whole country on 30 April 1975.

The victory of the Vietnamese people after these two wars was the victory of courage, bravery, and people's power unified under the leadership of Ho Chi Minh and the Communist Party of Vietnam. It was also the victory of international solidarity of peace and justice lovers from all over the world supporting the just cause of the Vietnamese people. In April 2010, on the 35th celebration of the liberation of the South and reunification of the country, many international friends came to join in the celebrations and rejoice with us and to once again affirm that the fight, sacrifice and the victory of the Vietnamese people made an important contribution to the cause of national liberation, for democracy and progress of many peoples all over the world. On our part, we remain always thankful and will never forget the valuable support and solidarity of peoples of the world with the liberation struggle of the Vietnamese people.

## A difficult decade after liberation

After the country was fully liberated in 1975, Vietnamese people had to undergo another decade of hardship.

The war left behind heavy consequences for Vietnam. Before the war, the colonial system impoverished most of the country. The war prevented our country from developing, destroying the country's infrastructure, environment and most seriously, killing millions of people, leaving millions of others homeless, parentless, invalids and victims of Agent Orange/dioxin. After the war, we badly needed a peaceful environment as well as resources, support and assistance to heal the wounds of war, rebuild the country and improve people's living conditions. But that did not happen. Vietnam had to go through another difficult period after the war.

The US imposed an economic embargo on Vietnam for nearly 20 years, launched many campaigns of sabotage and provocative actions, including supporting terrorist and separatist activities against Vietnam. The Khmer Rouge regime in Cambodia had already committed genocide against its own people, and began military attacks against Vietnam. As Vietnam helped the Cambodian people to get rid of and prevent the return to power of the Khmer Rouge in Cambodia, Western countries and their allies used this for the purpose of isolating and weakening Vietnam. The conflict and tensions along the Northern borders also took a heavy toll in human and material resources for Vietnam. The only limited assistance we received was from the Soviet Union and other socialist countries, but these countries also faced a difficult time and had not much help to offer. These objective factors significantly worsened the socio-economic situation in Vietnam in 1970s and 1980s.

There were also subjective reasons that further aggravated the situation. Soon after the country's reunification in 1976, Vietnam expanded a centrally planned economy based on the state and collective ownership on a nation-wide scale. All major means of production, factories and private companies were nationalized. Agricultural land belonged mainly to cooperatives and only 5% was distributed to peasants for individual family use. Small private and family production, without wage labor, was still allowed. Small shops and simple markets for direct sale were also in existence while all essential production materials and consumer goods were circulated through the state distribution system. This model brought about social equality but did not sufficiently develop the economy. Labor productivity was remarkably low. Even though we remained an agriculture-based nation, we still suffered from chronic food shortages. As a result, we had to import approximately one million tons of food annually. Other essential consumer goods were also lacking. The inflation rate skyrocketed in the 1980s, and reached a peak of 774%. The people's livelihoods were in very poor shape. We were, in fact, engulfed in a severe social-economic crisis.

We realized that apart from external unfavorable factors, we had made mistakes in prolonging a form of management of society and socio-economic development which worked well during times of war, but was no longer useful in the new context.

**On management:** The central planning mechanism, though useful in removing a number of negative aspects of the market economy, was not compatible with the current level of economic and management development. Comprehensive planning from the center, on the one hand cannot ensure the diverse and changing needs of the society, and on the other hand it limits the dynamic, innovative and creative features of the grassroots. Planning mainly through an administrative system creates 'a beg-and-give' mechanism, distorting real economic relations, and contributing to increasing bureaucratization of the economy.

**On ownership:** The universal application of state and collective ownership through the restricting of private ownership, abolishing the exploitative class system, does not conform to the existing level of development of productive forces in Vietnam. In reality, we oversocialized our productive relations while the level of development of productive forces was very low and it was against Marx's principle of development of the relations of production. As a result, this undermined the motivation to improve production and failed to mobilize resources in society for economic development while state resources remained very limited.

**On distribution:** The application of subsidies and egalitarian distribution systems, while ensuring equality amongst the population, created a "welfare state" in the worst meaning of this term, wherein everyone was entitled to jobs, free housing, free education and health care services, but the productive capacity was not up to fulfilling these goals and building society. In order to provide all these free services, the government had to use all available resources, which left little or no resources for development. As a result, everyone was equal, but equally poor and there was very limited capacity to improve living standards. At the same time, the egalitarian distribution together with collective ownership contributed to reduce the motivation to increase labor productivity, leading to notable waste in production and economic activities.

In a nutshell, the biggest shortcoming was that there was confusion between the desired objectives and current economic reality. We were too eager to apply achievements of socialism while still at the initial stage of the transition to socialism. The objectives of socialism are noble but achieving them requires adequate economic, material and technical conditions, as well as cultural development. It's a long-term process, not a one-day business and cannot be realized only by political will. In fact, we did not yet have socialism; we were at the beginning of the process of building it. And there is a need for suitable policies and steps relevant to the existing context and objective conditions.

## Doi Moi - The Renewal Process and the Socialist-oriented Market Economy

Since the mid-1980s, the Communist Party of Vietnam has initiated a renewal policy called in Vietnamese "Doi Moi" to correct the above shortcomings. Many elements of the "Doi Moi" policies originated from creative initiatives and successful experiments implemented in various localities and then supported by the Party's leadership. The 6th Party Congress in 1986 decided to officially bring this policy into reality. It immediately received wide and enthusiastic support from the whole society and had a positive impact on the overall situation in the country.

Regarding socio-economic development, the renewal policy was focused on the switch to a market economy with a socialist orientation. Vietnam's socialist-oriented market economy consists of the following features:

· To consider the market as a means for the liberation of productive forces for economic development and economic growth as a condition to achieve socialist development objectives. The market should be regulated by a socialist state in order to utilize its potentials and minimize its negative aspects, and to orient its functioning towards the realization of the socio-economic development objectives for the benefit of the whole society.

· The market should be combined with macro planning for rational distribution of resources, and to ensure the achievement of socio-economic development objectives in an integrated and consistent manner.

· As a mixed economy with the public economic sector playing the key role, productive relations should be developed gradually in accordance with the level of the development of the productive forces.

· As a sovereign, self-managed economy linked with widening international economic integration and cooperation, Vietnam should aim to maximize the utilization of domestic potential in combination with the rational use of external resources.

The development of a socialist-oriented market economy in Vietnam has brought about real positive changes for our country over the past two and half decades.

The economy has begun to grow. Gross Domestic Product (GDP) has increased at a fairly high rate, averaging at about 7-8 % per year during the past 25 years.

The economic structure of ownership was diversified to allow mobilization of additional resources for the country's development. The state sector plays a dominating role in the decisively important areas for the macro-economy such as energy, main natural resources, heavy industry and communication, railways, aviation and public transportation, in banking and insurance, etc.

The state sector also plays an active role in the areas that have significant impact on the interests of large social groups such as construction, production of fertilizer, construction materials and essential consumer goods, light industry, trading of agricultural products, etc. Gross Domestic Product output in 2008 is divided as follows: the state sector contributed 34%, the collective: 6%, the household: 30%, the national private: 11% and the foreign-invested sector: 19%. Workforce distribution according to ownership structure in 2009 is divided as follows: the state sector employed 10.5%, the collective: 0.3%, the national private and household: 85.8%, and the foreign-invested: 3.4%.

In Vietnam, agricultural land remains owned by the state but is distributed to peasants on a household basis for long-term use. New forms of cooperatives started to emerge gradually along with the development of the productive forces in agriculture on a voluntary basis. International economic cooperation has been expanded rapidly. The volume of foreign trade increased from 2-3 billion US Dollars (USD) per year in the 80s to 155 billion USD in 2010 while the country's exports increased from 1 billion USD to 71.6 billion USD in the same period. Vietnam's major trading partners in 2010 were China (27.3 bn. USD), ASEAN (20 bn. USD), USA (18 bn. USD), EU (17.7 bn. USD), Japan (16.7 bn. USD) and Korea (12.7 bn. USD). Foreign direct investment registered reached 192 billion USD in total by the end of 2010 with the largest investors coming from Taiwan (11.8%), Korea (11.5%), Singapore (11.3%), Japan (10.8%) and Malaysia (9.5%). Structure of total invested capital in 2010 in Vietnam is 39.4% from the state sector, 34.9% from local non-state resources, 22.6% from foreign resources and 3.1% from other resources. Remittances from Vietnamese living abroad have been increasing and reached 8 billion USD in 2010.

From being insufficient in food supply, Vietnam has satisfied its population's needs for food consumption and has started to export rice since the late 1980s. At present, Vietnam is the world's 2nd largest rice exporter and one of the world's largest exporters of a number of other agricultural products.

The industrial share of GDP has risen from 21.6% in 1988 to 41.1% in 2010 while agriculture went from 46.3% to 20.6%, and the service sector from 33.1% to 38.3% respectively. The labor force in agriculture has been reduced from 73.02% of the total workforce in 1990 to 48.2% in 2010, while industry and service increased their labor share from 12.1% to 22.4% and from 19.7% to 29.4% respectively during the period from 2000-2010.

Per capita GDP increased from 120 USD in 1986 to 1,168 USD in 2010. As such, according to UN criteria, Vietnam has stepped out of the underdeveloped country group in 2008. Regarding social development, the renewal policy comprises the following key elements:

· To place human beings at the center of development, and economic development as the facilitators of social development objectives. To ensure that social equality and progress goes hand-in-hand with every step of economic development.

· To enable all people to realize their potential and encourage them to increase their income and prosperity lawfully while the state and the whole society concentrate efforts on alleviating poverty, empowering the poor and assisting people in difficult circumstances.
· To regard education, training, science and technology as a prime national policy to develop human resources and a catalyst for sustainable social development.
· To place cultural development as foundation for advancement of the society. Vietnam in 2010 had a population of over 86 million people, 70% of them live in rural areas. The nation consists of 54 ethnic minority groups, the Kinh (Vietnamese) account for 85% of the population.

Economic growth has helped the country overcome the socio-economic crisis in the 1980s and visibly improved the people's living conditions.

The national program on agricultural and rural development, support for remote and distant areas, has been an important priority of the state and society. By 2008, over 99% of the villages had electricity (compared with 60.4% in 1994), 100% of villages had primary schools and 95% had junior secondary schools (compared with 76.6% in 1994), 100% of villages had telephone communication (compared with 82.6% in 1994), and 99% of the villages had health care centers.

Hunger eradication and poverty reduction constitute a supreme priority in the socio-economic development strategy. Many policies have been adopted, projects and programs implemented to support the poor, ethnic minorities, and people living in remote and distant areas, people with disabilities, and other people in difficult circumstances. The poverty rate has been brought down from 75% in 1986 to 58.1% in 1993, 37.4% in 1998, 29% in 2002, 25% in 2004, 19% in 2006, 16% in 2007, 13.5% in 2008 and 9.5% in 2010. According to the World Bank, poverty in Vietnam has been reduced by 2/3 from 1993 to 2006.

The state continues to play a leading role in the fields of education and healthcare. Vietnam has completed the goal of eliminating illiteracy, universalizing primary education by the year 2000, and according to plan, will achieve universal junior secondary education this year. Enrolment increased from 14.9 million in the 1994-1995 academic year to 23 million in the 2009-2010 academic year, while the university and college student population increased from 203,000 to 1.8 million in the same period. The number of community education centers has increased from 370 in the 2001-2002 academic year to 9,500 in the 2008-2009 academic year. Enrollment in informal regular education increased from 1.45 million to 12.2 million in the same period. By 2005, 95% of the adult population was literate. Government spending on education as a percent of the national budget accounted for 10% in 1986 and increased to 15% in 2000 and 20% in 2009.

Many epidemic diseases have been put under strict control. The state has issued free health insurance to the poor, people in difficult circumstances, and children under 6. The under-5 child malnutrition rate has gone down from 51% in 1995 to 18% in 2010. The maternal mortality rate has

*Schoolgirls CCDS met in Sapa*

been reduced four times from 233 to below 60 per 100,000 births. The average life expectancy increased from 62 years in 1990 to 72 years in 2007. The Gross National Income (GNI) index in 2006 was 0.36.

The country's Human Development Index (HDI) rose from 0.498 in 1991 to 0.688 in 2000 and 0.733 in 2007. The recent review by the United Nations has shown that Vietnam is a leading country in the world in the realization of Millennium Development Goals.

The fundamental characteristics of the Vietnamese political system are determined by the concrete historical development process in Vietnam and the socialist-oriented objectives of the country.

## Multi-Party System

Concerning the historical process, the political system formed after the August revolution was multi-party. The government headed by Ho Chi Minh initiated the first ever in the nation's history free and democratic election in which the communists received the utmost support of the people with an absolute majority of votes. There were some political parties that did not do well in the election, but in order to promote national unity, Ho Chi Minh convinced his colleagues to reserve 70 out of 403 seats for these parties in the National Assembly.

The invasion of the French and later the Americans had a deep impact in the political context of Vietnam. Some political parties took the side of the foreign invaders against their own people, and by doing so, excluded themselves from the political arena after the country was liberated. At the same time, the wise leadership of Ho Chi Minh and the Communist Party of Vietnam, and the examples of sacrifice of the communists for the country has brought the Communist party the utmost credibility. That is why the Vietnamese people usually call the Communist Party of Vietnam "Our Party". That's why it can be said that the leadership position of the Communist Party of Vietnam resulted from a practical, historic struggle of the Vietnamese people during the past 65 years.

On the other hand, building socialism is not a spontaneous but a self-conscious, oriented and long-term process towards achieving socialist objectives. The continuity and consistency of the political leadership therefore is inevitable and vitally important for socialist construction. Vietnam is trying to develop a political system using a form of organization and management of society based on the principle of "social consensus", not "centralization" (such as dictatorship, totalitarianism, etc.), or "decentralization" (such as political opposition and competition, etc.). This is possible since socialist society is a values-oriented society striving for common interests and objectives and not a society where various groups and individuals are competing for their own interests, which always results in the domination and exploitation by a richer minority of the majority of society.

Vietnam's political system consists of the leadership of the Communist Party, the management of the people's state, and the master role of the people united through social consensus based on common objectives and interests.

Today's Communist Party of Vietnam comprises more than 3 million members with a network rooted to the grassroots in all localities. Vietnam is now in the process of building a rule-based socialist state of the people, by the people and for the people. The National Assembly is the supreme legislative body and is elected every five years through a popular vote based on a direct and secret ballot. The National Assembly executes the supreme legislative and supervisory power related to the operations of state organs. The National Assembly's lively discussion sessions on the most important issues and hearings are broadcast on television and radio across the country.

Thousands of diverse people's organizations have developed across the country, including the Vietnam Fatherland Front, mass socio-political organizations, social, professional and non-governmental organizations. Media agencies have developed rapidly and are playing an active and important role in the political life of the country, providing information to the people, reflecting public opinions and fighting against bureaucratization and corruption. At present, Internet users account for about 25% of the total population.

All citizens are entitled to freedom of religion including the freedom to practice no religion. Nowadays, there are about 10 million Buddhists, 6 million Catholics, 800 thousand Protestants, 2.5 million Cao Dai believers, 2 million Hoa Hao followers, and 70,000 Muslims. In addition, most Vietnamese are practitioners of traditional ancestral worship. The number of newly-built pagodas and churches, as well as the number of new followers have increased notably in the recent years.

Women's role and status has kept improving in the society. At present, Vietnam has 25.8% women's representation in the National Assembly (the Parliament). About 17% of the total deputies are from ethnic minorities. The implementation of "Grassroots Democracy" over the past decade has enabled more and more people to have direct participation and a major role in their localities across the country.

## On International Relations

In the current international context, maintaining a peaceful and stable environment and cooperation for development is in the interests

of all nations. Vietnam stands for a foreign policy of independence, self-determination, diversification and multi-lateralization of international relations. We stand for developing friendly, equal, and mutually beneficial cooperative relationships with all countries, with a particular focus on our neighbors and countries in the region, and at the same time contributing to the common struggle of the world's people for peace, national independence, and for democracy and social progress.

Under the motto "Shelving the past, looking towards the future," Vietnam has normalized relations with formerly "hostile' countries." Vietnam became a member of the United Nations in 1976, normalized relations with China in 1991, with the USA in 1995, joined the Association of Southeast Asia Nations (ASEAN) in 1995, the Asia-Europe Meeting (ASEM) in 1996, Asia-Pacific Economic Cooperation (APEC) in 1998 and WTO in 2006. Nowadays, Vietnam maintains friendly and good cooperative relations with all countries in the region, having diplomatic relations with 180 countries around the world. Vietnam considers itself to be a friend and reliable partner with all countries in the world community, developing relations with all countries, territories, and international organizations, based on key principles. These principles are respect for independence, sovereignty, territorial integrity, non-interference in internal affairs, no use of force or threat of using force, settlement of disagreements and disputes through peaceful negotiations, mutual respect, and equal and mutual beneficial cooperation . While diversifying foreign relationships, Vietnam has been consistently consolidating and strengthening its ties with traditional friends and countries of the South. Vietnam has always supported Cuba, is in solidarity with the people of Palestine, and just causes of people around the world, and actively participating in the Non-Aligned Movement for a world of peace and justice.

## Challenges and Tasks

Vietnam is undergoing deep and multi-dimensional transitional processes, including the following:

"Transition from an underdeveloped and agriculture-based country to an industrialized and modernized economy in the context of globalization, competition and the global crises of energy, ecology and climate change.

"Transition from a centrally-planned to a market economy with a socialist orientation.

"Transition from a command system to the formation of a rule-of-law socialist state.

"Transition from a relatively closed society to an open one, including integration into a fast changing world with increasing inequality, challenges and multiple crises.

On top of this, Vietnam strives to find an unprecedented path to construct a new type society - a socialist society - through a market economy, opening-up and having international integration in the world dominated by capitalism. It is not an easy task. Despite encouraging achievements, Vietnam is still far away from the society that we desire. There are many limitations and weaknesses we need to overcome.

With regard to economic development, Vietnam is still a poor country with a relatively low level of productive forces, poor infrastructure, low quality human resources and insufficient market management capacity. The market-led elements in economic growth caused serious limitations in the quality and sustainability of development. The hard and unequal competition in the unjust international economic order and the increasing dependence on external markets and resources pose a permanent challenge to the country's macro-economy and economic sovereignty. The state economic sector is also under threat due to its low efficiency and weak management while competing with other growing sectors. Vietnam is one of the countries suffering the most from the impact of natural disasters and climate change.

The XI Congress of the Communist Party of Vietnam placed an emphasis on the quality and sustainability of development with special focus on the improvement of the market management and administrative system, the quality of human resources and infrastructure in the forthcoming period. Our tasks are also to develop national progressive productive forces, to ensure economic sovereignty and the effectiveness of the state sector as the leading actor in the economy. The general goal for Vietnam is to become an industrialized country with a modern character by 2020 with per capita GDP of 3000 USD.

Concerning social development, aside from numerous achievements, there are still many problem and challenges. The legacy of war is still heavy in the country. Part of the population continues to remain poor; living conditions and interests of many working people are not yet appropriately met; disparities are rising. Quality of education, healthcare and the number of public services remain limited. The negative impacts of the market economy and the opening-up of the economy continue to damage our system of social and ethical values;

consumerism and individualism is spreading and social evils are becoming more complicated.

The XI Congress of the Communist Party of Vietnam (CPV) set tasks to continue reducing poverty, further improve people's living standards and quality of education and health care, promote social equality and progress, reinforce ethical values and the cultural foundation of the society. The basic goal is to reduce poverty by 2% annually, to lift the real income of people 3.5 times, to raise the average life expectancy to 75 years and to lift the Human Development Index (HDI) into the upper group in the medium level of the world's countries by 2020.

With regard to politics, an external challenge is that there are outside forces who continue to use the pretext of "democracy and human rights" to sabotage Vietnam, using "peaceful evolution" as well as religious and ethnic conflicts to penetrate and destabilize the political situation and undermine the socialist-oriented course of Vietnam. The main internal challenge is bureaucratization and corruption, ideological disorientation and ethical degradation that could lead to the weakening of the socialist orientation in the country's political foundation as well as people's relationship with the Party.

The XI CPV Congress therefore considered that a key task is to enhance the leadership capacity and militancy of the Party, to strive for purity, solidity and effectiveness of the political system. There is a need also to improve democratic institutions and processes for strengthening people's participation and consolidating the ties between the Party, State and the people and to reinforce national unity in the cause of achieving the common objective of building a country with a prosperous people, strong nation, and a democratic, equitable and civilized society.

## Conclusion

Socialist objectives can be shared commonly but roads to socialism can vary, based on concrete subjective and objective conditions. Our Renewal course is an effort to find a new way towards socialism within the concrete situation of Vietnam. Building socialism through a market economy and opening-up means accepting an open and direct struggle between socialism and capitalism in all economic, social, political, ideological and cultural aspects of daily life of society. And socialist-oriented development means a continuing process of consolidation and strengthening socialist factors in all those areas in a consistent and integrated manner, making them prevail and at some stage, making them irreversible in the society. This is a new and very challenging task, especially in today's world situation. The correct leadership by the Party and support by the people are the most important and decisive factors in this process.

We do believe that our chosen path is just and pertinent to the interests of the Vietnamese people. This is reflected in the fact that Vietnamese have been ranking among the highest in the international survey on people's optimism over the past years. In April, 2010, on the occasion of the 35th anniversary of the country's reunification, the Associated Press collaborated with GfK Poll to conduct a survey among ordinary people in Vietnam and came to the conclusion that "Vietnamese people are happy with their revolutionary achievements", with 85% of those surveyed saying that the economy is developing, 87% believing it will continue to develop, and 81% feel the country is on the right track.

The achievements of the renewal over the past 25 years in Vietnam have shown that socialist-oriented development is possible, is viable, and is necessary for our people, especially in today's context of global crises.

# Chapter 5. Vietnam Update 2013: Opportunities and Challenges

## By Merle Ratner and Ngo Thanh Nhan

The proceeding chapters in this book capture the reality of Vietnam today as a dynamic country that has made historic progress in poverty alleviation, women's rights and consistently improving the lives of its people. Doing all this in the context of a monumental struggle towards independence, reunification and socialism makes these achievements more impressive still.

Yet building socialism in a world dominated by predatory and rapacious capitalism is not easy.

*A younger Ho Chi Minh*

The socialist-oriented market economy Vietnam has chosen contains within it great contradictions that are increasingly coming to the fore as Vietnam's successes in development spawn both heightened expectations and dangers. Tran Dac Loi's paper eloquently describes the trajectory of Vietnam's development in the post-war period, outlining the successes and contradictions. In the past year, some of these contradictions have ripened, creating the possibility for the Communist Party to make necessary changes. At the same time, if the weaknesses identified are not remedied, the revolution risks losing the overwhelming support that it maintains among the people.

The Vietnamese Communist Party has faced many obstacles and threats throughout its long history. One of the hallmarks of the Party has been its ability to discover, evaluate and correct its errors. In the few years since Tran Dac Loi's paper was written, widespread public discussion in Vietnam has highlighted popular concerns about something that President Ho Chi Minh often warned about - a decline in the revolutionary morality within the Party. Simply put, there is increasing public anger at the growing corruption, opportunism and conspicuous consumption of a relatively small but powerful sector of the Party and government, especially in the face of a slowdown in the economy affecting people's lives. (The rate of inflation has recently been cut to less than 10% which is a positive trend, but Vietnam has been somewhat affected by the international economic crisis.)

Current concerns are compounded by the perception that the government is mired in bureaucracy and doesn't sufficiently serve the people. This is particularly urgent in health care and education, which, while available in all areas, comes with increasing fees attached and reduced quality for those who cannot pay more. Extremely poor people do get free medical care and scholarships and the fact that every grass roots area has basic services is praiseworthy. But, as doctors and teachers were allowed to teach/practice privately after their state jobs to make ends meet, a two tier system has developed with better care for those with money.

Peasants are negatively affected by urbanization and the shortage (and reallocation) of farmland. Many workers still face poor working conditions and wages, particularly in the private and foreign invested sector. They do benefit from a very strong labor law, with the absolute right to organize a union and strike, but labor unions are struggling to adjust from state to private sector conditions. Because of the growing gap between the rich and the poor, many of those who sacrificed everything for the revolution during the war, particularly those in the guerrilla forces are now facing hardships.

## Contradictions between Socialism and Capitalism

These contradictions have raised questions about the theory of socialist development in Vietnam and have sometimes led to unfortunate proposals. The theory that state control over the primary productive centers would be the anchor for socialist development, as detailed by Duncan McFarland, is being undermined by scandals in the management of the state owned enterprises. The Party's decision to allow members to own businesses and business owners to become members raises issues about the role of the Party as the vanguard of the working class and the primacy of fighting exploitation of the working class. Issues of land usage and development, particularly seizures of land by certain corrupt local governments, have prompted some Party members to call for private ownership of land as a means of protecting peasants' land rights - something that we believe would be disastrous for Vietnam's independence and socialist future. The Communist Party has wisely decided to maintain the ownership of land by the whole people. The "noisy" push for privatization of land, even with the open support of the US government, has not been successful.

*Vo Thi Thang, student organizaer against the US in the South*

Ironically, some of those who correctly target the problems of corruption and opportunism confuse the cause and effect, incorrectly assigning societal achievements to the market and blaming the socialist mechanism for the negative phenomena.

This is a mistake, since whatever the use of the market mechanism and private production in raising production and providing more necessary goods to the people, it was, and is, the socialist distributive mechanism and the leadership of the Party and people that has resulted in the gains in standard of living still being enjoyed by the majority of the masses.

## Stopping Corruption is Key to Success

The Communist Party has identified the struggle against corruption and negative social phenomenon internally as one of its highest priorities. Senior state officials have been called to account in the National Assembly and even on TV for their mistakes and misdeeds.

The masses in Vietnam continue to be active in asserting their rights to what the Vietnamese call collective mastery. Often led by revolutionary heroes of the struggle against the US, peasants demonstrate and take militant action against illegal land seizures and other forms of corruption. Some of these struggles have been successful in returning the illegally taken land.

Workers organize thousands of strikes a year, the majority of them wildcat strikes against privately owned companies that have partial or full foreign ownership. Most of these strikes result in at least partial victories for the workers, something we can only dream about in the US at this time.

The Vietnamese constitution is now in the process of being amended, with massive popular input. By initiating this society-wide discussion, the Communist Party is implementing grass roots democracy and showing its confidence in Vietnam's path to socialism. The current draft gives more rights to the grass roots, rights to welfare and employment, provides a clearer balance of powers between the President, the Prime Minister, and the National Assembly, and maintains a clear commitment to building socialism.

If the Communist Party majority and the masses are successful in dislodging the small but entrenched core of corruption, the country will be able to continue to push forward on its transition to socialism with dynamism, creativity and enthusiasm. If the corruption is not sufficiently checked, then two things may result: bourgeois elements with foreign support will take the opportunity to regroup in opposition, and some honest Party members may, in desperation, forsake socialism for some illusory capitalist alternative.

The Vietnamese people, who defeated Chinese, French, Japanese and US domination, colonialism and imperialism, are up for this fight and will not abandon their determination to build an independent socialist society. Vietnam has a history of being able to use its many strengths to correct its shortcomings. We are confident that the Party and the people of Vietnam will weather this storm as they have weathered many others and will emerge with a country "ten times more beautiful," as Ho Chi Minh said.

# Chapter 6. Origins of the 'Doi Moi' Policy in Vietnam and the Relationship to Lenin's New Economic Policy

## By Duncan McFarland

In 1975 Vietnam celebrated the historic victory over US imperialism in the American War. After more than 110 years of struggle against French colonialism, Japanese imperialism and the US, the Vietnamese again secured national independence. The cause championed by Ho Chi Minh resulted in victory, the latest chapter in Vietnam's 2000 year history of fighting for independence.

Shifting from war to peace-time work, the Vietnam-ese faced a daunting set of tasks: national reconciliation and reconstruction, interna-tional integration and building

*Playing soccer near Lenin statue.*

socialism. It is necessary to consider the extremely difficult situa-tion then facing Vietnam. After 40 years of almost continuous war, including the large-scale and particularly brutal campaign waged by the US, there was a huge amount of destruction in the country. Most of the villages in the South and the cities in the North had been heav-ily bombed, with bridges, railroads and factories destroyed.

The total number of bombs dropped by the US on Vietnam was great-er than the US dropped in all theaters during World War II. Some 3-4 million Vietnamese people were killed in the war. Ignoring international law, the US waged the largest chemical war in history using Agent Orange and other defoliants, making much agricultural land unusable.

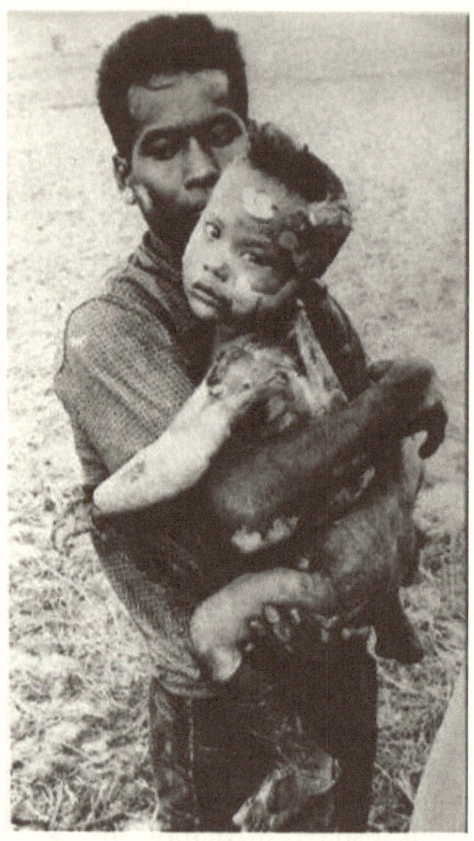

There were major population shifts, with peasants fleeing the countryside and migrations from one region to another. Many families were divided. Some one million soldiers needed reintegration into civilian life. Many thousands of political prisoners were released from jail. The large South Vietnam/US military and government apparatus had to be dismantled. US war policy had deliberately exacerbated tensions among Vietnam's numerous ethnic and religious groups, including the creation of militias which had to be disarmed. The US further reneged on its financial commitments to support reconstruction, specified as part of the Paris Peace Accords; instead, the US organized an international economic boycott to isolate Vietnam from the world market. The sudden withdrawal of massive US aid to the Saigon regime and the South led to unemployment and shortages of goods.

Such were the gigantic challenges. Yet, the prestige of the Communist Party of Vietnam (CPV) in leading the effort to defeat US imperialism was high, people's enthusiasm great, and a new government of a united Vietnam formed in Hanoi. Saigon was renamed Ho Chi Minh City. The Soviet Union gave food aid, numerous Western governments granted diplomatic recognition, and Vietnam was admitted to the United Nations. The "bloody revenge" predicted by US propagandists never materialized. Basic steps to restore order and normalcy were achieved.

The Fourth Congress of the CPV met in December 1976 to decide on the plan of socialist economic development. The Vietnamese Communist Party was understandably impressed with the achievements of the Soviet Union and had a very negative impression of capitalism, based on Vietnam's experiences with French colonialism and US capitalism and imperialism. The CPV Congress adopted an advanced socialist model based on the USSR: it had a high level of centralized planning, emphasis on heavy industry and collectivized farming, and suppressed private production. Thus, Vietnam began its journey to communism.

## Hardships Lead to Crisis

Negative international developments soon put great pressure on the new government. Border attacks from the Khmer Rouge in Cambodia led to Vietnamese troops defeating the Khmer Rouge and its leader, Pol Pot, and occupying Cambodia to help restore normalcy. A short but bloody border war was fought in the north and there were ongoing tensions with Vietnam's huge northern neighbor. Thus, large amounts of resources needed for domestic construction were still tied up in the military.

The Fourth Communist Party of Vietnam Congress approved ambitious plans for economic development, but the targets were not met. Industrial production stagnated and food production fell short of population growth. Serious inflation proved a persistent problem and a black market emerged because of unmet needs. An unwieldy bureaucratic apparatus was unable to respond to problems. There was a general lack of personnel trained in economic management and professional skills of all sorts. Corruption among officials was a serious issue. All of these things contributed to rising dissatisfaction among the people.

The Fifth Party Congress in 1982 made criticisms and some adjustments, but did not basically alter the situation. State revenues and the balance of trade were in deficit, wages insufficient for workers to live and a system of rationing was implemented. A re-issue of increasingly devalued currency in September 1985 was counterproductive and inflation surged. The state began to import rice to deal with increasing hunger.

A general feeling of crisis became pervasive and provided the context of the Sixth Party Congress in 1986. The program of the Fourth Party Congress was reevaluated: while social services for the people were guaranteed for all by the government, they were underfunded, and there were no resources for investment. There was much spirited debate with an emphasis on facing the plain facts: on most counts, the government's economic policies were a failure.

The Political Report of the Sixth CPV Congress made criticisms, referring to "very serious errors in economic leadership and management in the last five years." For example, measures taken regarding wages, prices, currency and distribution of commodities were enacted without proper preparation and "did not fit the actual situation." In general, the adopted socialist system was much too advanced for the low level of economic development. Who was responsible? "The Central Committee, the Politburo, the Secretariat and the Council of Ministers were primarily responsible for the above mentioned mistakes and shortcomings in Party leadership," the CPV Congress concluded in a frank admittance of leadership mistakes.

## New Policies Embraced and the NEP

New measures were adopted. Truong Chinh, the General Secretary of the Communist Party, termed the new economic policy "Doi Moi" or renewal. The overemphasis on centralized management, heavy industry and cooperative agriculture would be changed in the new system, balancing state control of key sectors with greater decen-

tralization and reintroduction of the market and a private economy. Foreign investment would be encouraged in export-oriented manufacture. The state retained control of heavy industry, energy, finance and media while encouraging the expansion of a state regulated market in small and light industry. Agricultural land would be contracted to individual families for a 15 year period.

This was a mixed economy with socialist and capitalist sectors, with socialism in control, called a socialist oriented market economy. Vietnam was in a period of transition to socialism, with the full construction of a socialist society seen as a long and difficult process. After the adoption of Doi Moi, the economy rebounded quickly, especially in agriculture. By 1989, Vietnam was exporting one million tons of rice per year.

The comparisons to the New Economic Policy (NEP) adopted by the Soviet Union in 1920 were striking. Russia was a largely undeveloped country that had experienced major losses during World War I. That was followed by two years of a destructive civil war, made worse by the military intervention by 17 foreign countries intent on overthrowing the young socialist state. The Bolshevik leaders successfully implemented a centralized, command economy, "war communism," during the civil war period. For peacetime reconstruction, however, war communism proved a disaster; famine emerged along with opposition to Bolshevik power. Lenin's response was to reintroduce the free market in the countryside and in light industry, while retaining Bolshevik control of the "commanding heights" of heavy industry, the financial system, and foreign trade. The NEP proved effective in rehabilitating the Soviet economy in the 1920s.

## Results of Doi Moi

With the Doi Moi policy and the creation of the socialist-oriented market economy, Vietnam's economy recovered rapidly. For the past twenty-five years, Vietnam's rate of growth of GDP has been among the fastest in the world. It has been a period of great changes in the economy and society. Although poverty still exists in Vietnam, most working people have a better income and a higher standard of living. Vietnam's poverty alleviation program has been very successful and received awards from the United Nations. Basic education and healthcare are available for most people and stores in the cities are stocked with consumer goods. Vietnam has expanding foreign trade, diplomatic relations with most countries and is active in international organizations such as the Association of Southeast Asian Nations.

These are remarkable achievements for a country devastated by war and not long ago considered one of the worlds poorest. However,

*Doi Moi has increased prosperity*

these accomplishments have brought a new set of troubling problems. Integration into an international community dominated by global capitalism challenges Vietnam's socialist orientation and independence, since the largest capitalist powers and corporations strive to dominate the world economy by control of financial resources, markets and natural resources. Income disparities have increased in Vietnam along with exploitation. Industrial development has damaged the environment. The high level of collectivity and moral standards of the revolution have eroded; endemic bureaucracy and corruption has generated cynicism among some people. Methods of teaching Marxism must be improved. Inflation has been a serious problem, especially after the great global recession of 2008, but has now been brought down to less than seven percent.

Consequently, the Communist Party of Vietnam and government have major challenges on the path towards socialism, as problems assume increasingly complex cultural and ideological forms in the global context. It is very difficult to create sustainable, socialist-oriented growth starting from poverty and lack of development. However, Vietnam has time and again overcome seemingly insurmountable obstacles to create a better future for the Vietnamese people. In an era of deteriorating capitalism, progressives need to support the construction of socialism in Vietnam as a shining example for the world of humanity's hope and future.

# Chapter 7. United States Foreign Policy and the War in Vietnam

## By Harry R. Targ

The United States began its involvement in Vietnam right after World War II by funding the French effort to reestablish its colonial empire in Indochina. The United States sought to construct a post-war world order that would maximize its economic and geopolitical interests on a global level. This meant challenging the Soviet Union, the Communist revolution in China, and national liberation and socialist movements all across the Global South. Along with its global anti-Communist agenda, corporate and banking interests originally intent on advancing the US presence in Europe and maintaining US hegemony in Latin America, advocated policies to get a foothold in Asia to exploit its resources, as well as those of its neighbors, Cambodia and Laos, collectively referred to as Indochina, and all of Southeast Asia. From the very beginning, it was an imperialist relationship.

After the onset of the civil war on the Korean Peninsula in 1950, the United States concerned itself increasingly with the entire Third World. The peoples of Asia, Africa, and Latin America were actively opposing colonialism and neocolonialism. European and US imperialism in the Third World required markets, resources, cheap labor, and investment sites for profit making. To Europeans in Africa, and US interests in Asia, national liberation meant the threat of an end to foreign control of indigenous economies. The best opportunity for international capital, then, required continued opposition to anti-colonial struggles (as in Indochina, Algeria, Kenya, Ghana, Malaya, etc.) and opposition to movements challenging neocolonialism (as in the Philippines, Guatemala, Iran, and Egypt).

### The French Indochina War

The United States continued its commitment to the reactionary forces in Vietnam. Vietnam had been a colony of France since 1859.

During World War II the French collaborated with the Japanese, who had occupied Vietnam. After the Japanese had surrendered at the close of the war, the nationalist and Communist-led Vietminh forces controlled much of the country, and Ho Chi Minh, the movement leader, issued a declaration of independence. The French returned and sought to reestablish their dominance of the country. After the French attempted to achieve full control of Vietnam by means of negotiations, war broke out in 1946 and continued until 1954. The French formed their own "Republic of Vietnam" in June, 1948, and appointed the aristocrat collaborationist Bao Dai as leader of the new state. The Bao Dai regime was opposed by a broad front of political forces, of which Ho Chi Minh's Communists were in the lead. The Communist-led movement had the unqualified support of the Vietnamese people.

In February, 1950, the United States recognized the Bao Dai regime. In May, Truman's Secretary of State Dean Acheson called for the support of the French war effort in Vietnam, and an aid package was announced on June 27, after the Korean War had begun. From 1950 to 1954 the United States funded eighty percent of the cost of the French war. The Vietnamese people were increasingly supported by fraternal allies in the Socialist world. As Nguyen Khac Vien, who wrote a classic English language history of Vietnam pointed out: "The victory of the Chinese revolution and the founding of the People's Republic of China gave strong impetus to the Vietnamese resistance.... Early in 1950, the Democratic Republic of Viet Nam was accorded recognition by the People's Republic of China, the USSR and then by other socialist countries. From then on Viet Nam was no longer as isolated as it had been up to that point."[1]

## French Defeat by 1953

The French were losing their war in Vietnam by 1953 to the Vietnamese people. The new President Eisenhower told the American people that financial support for the French was needed to stop communism and support democracy in Vietnam. But, Eisenhower told a conference of US state governors meeting in Seattle on August 4, 1953 the real reasons for US involvement:

> "Now let us assume that we lost Indochina...The tin and tungsten that we so greatly value from that area would cease coming...So when the United States votes to give 400 million dollars to help that war, we are not voting for a give-away program. We are voting for the cheapest way that we can to prevent the occurrence

of something that would be of a most terrible significance to the United States of America, our security, our power and ability to get certain things we need from the riches of the Indochinese territory and from Southeast Asia."[2]

In February, 1954, France and other nations agreed to plan a conference at Geneva to discuss the continuing civil war. To improve their bargaining position the French simultaneously began an offensive by landing twenty thousand troops at the northern outpost of Dien Bien Phu. Within two months the French post was near capture.

## Domino Theory

During this last phase of the French war, the Eisenhower administration was seriously considering increased support for the French. Admiral Radford, head of the Joint Chiefs of Staff, called for the use of atomic weapons in keeping with the Dulles strategy of "massive retaliation" to defend the losing French effort. Dulles proclaimed that "communist domination" of Indochina and Southeast Asia would be a "grave threat to the whole free community." Eisenhower talked of "falling dominoes": if Indochina fell, then so would Burma, Thailand, Malaya, Indonesia, then India, Australia, New Zealand, the Philippines, Taiwan, and Japan as a series of falling dominoes. Vice President Nixon said on April 17, 1954:

> "The United States as a leader of the free world cannot afford further retreat in Asia. It is hoped the United States will not have to send troops there, but if this government cannot avoid it, the Administration must face up to the situation and dispatch forces."[3]

Dulles and Radford met with members of Congress in late April to discuss US air and troop support for the French, who were on the verge of surrender at Dien Bien Phu. The congressional leaders said they would support the military commitment only if the British would cooperate. When Dulles conferred with the British, the latter claimed that an act of intervention just shortly before the Geneva conference would be counterproductive. Thus, the U.S. drive toward intervention was temporarily stalled.

The Geneva Conference on Indochina opened on May 8. 1954 the same day that Dien Bien Phu fell to the forces of Ho Chi Minh. The signatories to the July, 1954, conference accords recognized the independence of Laos and Cambodia, temporarily split Vietnam at the Seventeenth Parallel, called for elections throughout Vietnam to occur by June, 1956 to reunite Vietnam under one government, and agreed not to introduce outside military force into the temporarily divided country. The United States did not sign the accords but agreed to honor them if the signatories did. Dulles's displeasure with the conference and with the need to meet with representatives from the People's Republic of China was evidenced by his personal withdrawal in the middle of the conference. The Vietnamese were reluctant to accept the partition of their country but realized the division would provide a base in the north for the full liberation of it in the future.

General Vo Nguyen Giap concluded about the end of the French Indo China War: "Our people and army have defeated a powerful and well-equipped enemy because our compatriots and our troops were motivated by a firm determination to fight for and win national independence, for the distribution of land to peasants, for peace, and for socialism. The enemy confronted a united front from all social classes and all political and religious affiliations....We are, moreover, living in an era in which the imperialists can no longer dominate completely."[4]

## Eisenhower Violates the Geneva Accords

After the conference the Eisenhower administration exerted pressure on former emperor Bao Dai and the French to install a hand-picked client, Ngo Dinh Diem, to serve as South Vietnam's new prime minister. Diem, who had lived in the United States from 1950 to 1953, was a friend of Cardinal Spellman, Senator John F. Kennedy, Supreme Court Justice William O. Douglas, and other US notables. In the fall of 1954, President Eisenhower sent his famous letter to Diem promising US military and economic assistance to South Vietnam if the government would carry out social reforms.

One year after the Geneva accords were signed, the US-financed puppet Diem announced that South Vietnam would not participate in negotiations for the holding of elections throughout Vietnam. He claimed that no elections in North Vietnam would be free.

President Eisenhower, years later, admitted the real reasons for calling off the 1956 elections in Vietnam. In his book Mandate for Change, he wrote: "I have never talked or corresponded with a person knowledgeable in Indochinese affairs who did not agree that had elections been held...possibly 80 per cent of the population would have voted for the Communist Ho Chi Minh."

In October, 1955, Diem ousted Bao Dai from his honorific post as chief of state. Diem installed several members of his family in military, police and political positions. The Diem family assumed ultimate power in South Vietnam. One analyst said that the United States had its Syngman Rhee (a right-wing puppet for the US in South Korea) for South Vietnam. The US Military Assistance Advisory Group then assumed full responsibility for training the South Vietnamese Army, contrary to the Geneva accords. South Vietnam was a creation in 1949 by the French colonial powers, and in 1954, after the Geneva Accords, by US imperial power. Both the French and US governments wanted to divide and weaken Vietnam by creating a client state in the south.

While the United States was replacing the French in South Vietnam, Secretary of State Dulles was expanding a network of alliances with client states around the world. The United States had already established a twenty-one-nation Western Hemispheric alliance, guaranteeing mutual consultation if any nation was attacked. NATO, created in 1949, represented fifteen north Atlantic and Mediterranean nations. The United States had joined in alliance with New Zealand and Australia. Finally, Dulles organized the South East Asia Treaty Organization (SEATO) in September, 1954, to counter the advance of communism that he saw as the result of the Geneva accords. Member countries were Britain, France, Australia, New Zealand, the Philippines, Thailand, Pakistan, and the United States.

The SEATO Treaty called for the protection of the Indochinese states, despite the fact that the latter were not members. Several Asian states, including India, refused to participate in the SEATO pact. Later, Dulles was to add the Baghdad Pact, or CENTO, as an alliance of client states in the Middle East. The United States also had treaty commitments to nations on a bilateral basis. All together, the United States had committed itself to the defense of at least fifty-four nations by the mid-1950s, all capitalist countries. Many were dependent on US financial aid, and all were committed to assisting the business interests of major US multinational corporations and banks.

From 1957 to 1960 a rapid escalation of violence occurred in South Vietnam as Diem sought to crush his growing opposition. During 1957-58, the United States entirely funded the Vietnamese armed forces, eighty percent of other government expenditures, and ninety percent of its imports. The Diem regime failed to carry out land reforms, and the countryside continued to be controlled by a small number of landlords. The repression against opposition of various political tendencies led finally to the formation of the National Liberation Front (NLF), in December, 1960, to oust the ruthless Diem regime, which maintained itself in power solely through U.S. support.

*Mass protest against Diem regime*

The US interest in the Third World in the 1960s is most brutally exemplified by its growing involvement in the Vietnam War. During the Eisenhower years the United States replaced the French as the predominant colonial power in South Vietnam. What later became referred to as "America's commitment" resulted from the U.S. statement of respect for the Geneva Accords, the Eisenhower promise to aid Diem, the commitment to the security of Indochina in the SEATO treaty written by the US, and the full-scale military assistance received by Diem from 1955.

## The Vietnam War Escalates

Kennedy acknowledged the escalating civil war in South Vietnam shortly upon taking office. Vice-President Johnson was sent to South Vietnam in May, 1961, to assess the progress of the counter guerrilla war there. He recommended that the United States continue its support to the Diem regime: "The basic question in South East Asia is here. We must decide whether to help these countries to the best of our ability or throw in the towel in the area and pull back our defenses to San Francisco and a 'Fortress America' concept. More important, we would say to the world in this case that we don't live up to treaties and don't stand by our friends."[5]

The new president as a senator had been a leading advocate for the South Vietnamese regime in the 1950s. Both he and his Vice President Lyndon Johnson had strongly supported "containing" communism - as did practically all political leaders, both Republicans and Democrats. Since the fight in Vietnam was framed as a fight to stop communism, most politicians and corporate and financial elites supported United States military involvement in Vietnam from the time of their betrayal of the Geneva Accords. The Vietnamese liberation struggle against the US-Diem regime escalated in response to the South Vietnamese regime's "policy of systematic terror against the entire southern population."[6] In late December, 1960, Vietnamese resistance fighters from the South met and established the National Liberation Front (NLF) to overthrow Diem, create a coalition government in the South, end all foreign intervention, and work towards establishing a peaceful reunification of all of Vietnam.

The Kennedy administration in the spring, 1961 added four hundred Special Forces troops to the contingent in South Vietnam and one hundred civilian advisors to aid in setting up the "strategic hamlet" program, designed to move peasant villagers away from areas influenced by NLF forces. In the fall of 1961 General Maxwell Taylor, head of the Joint Chiefs of Staff, and Walt Rostow, foreign policy advisor to the president, were sent to South Vietnam to study the situation. They returned recommending the introduction of U.S. ground troops, advice that was endorsed by Secretary of State Dean Rusk and Secretary of Defense Robert McNamara. Rusk and McNamara argued that the "fall" of South Vietnam would be a prelude to the "fall" of the rest of Southeast Asia and Indonesia - meaning falling away from the orbit of US control. A "loss" in Vietnam would also create a right-wing backlash within the United States, much like the backlash that followed the "fall of China."

With these recommendations, the Kennedy administration began a gradual escalation of direct U. S. involvement in the South Vietnamese civil war.  U.S. troop strength went from several hundred to ten thousand by 1963.  Meanwhile, the stability of the Diem government was declining.  The strategic hamlet program was generating recruits for the NLF, since it was disrupting life in the countryside.  Casualties among the South Vietnamese army and government officials grew. Opposition from Buddhists and students to Diem's harsh rule was becoming more intense.

*Buddhist monk immolating himself*

On May 8, 1963, the army shot into a nonviolent Buddhist demonstration. Buddhists later committed suicide in public protest against the Diem regime. In August, 1963, the South Vietnamese police and military invaded Buddhist pagodas and schools and arrested many dissidents. After a visit to Vietnam in September, 1963, McNamara and Taylor claimed that the United States would be able to end its involvement in the country by 1965. The head of the Military Assistance Advisory Group, General Harkins, predicted in November, 1963, that victory was just months away.

While these optimistic assessments were being made, as they were to be made throughout the war, opposition to Diem within the Vietnamese ruling clique itself was growing. South Vietnamese generals were ready to oust Diem. U.S. officials in South Vietnam disagreed in their evaluations of Diem's chances to maintain control of the country. Some U.S officials, like former Ambassador Frederick Nolting, were personal friends of Diem and remained committed to him, while others, such as the then-acting ambassador, Henry Cabot Lodge, and members of the CIA were opposed.

Finally, on November 1, 1963, with the support of Lodge and the CIA, Diem was overthrown by the South Vietnamese military, and one of the generals assumed office. This was to be the first of eleven governments during the remainder of South Vietnamese history. In the midst of the turmoil in South Vietnam, John Kennedy was assassinated in Dallas on November 22, 1963.

At the time of his death, there were fifteen thousand US troops in South Vietnam, a dramatic increase from the Eisenhower commitment but a small amount compared with what was to follow shortly. Troop commitments during the Kennedy administration were small, but Kennedy and his advisors established the military infrastructure, mobilized the academic expertise, and communicated an official rationale for escalating the U.S. struggle against the Third World. Military intervention was coupled with policies designed to encourage "economic development." While Kennedy was wrestling with what to do about Vietnam shortly before his death, the impression he wished to leave with the world was that the interests of the United States and the Third World were in fact identical. The Vietnamese people were experiencing just the opposite.

## President Johnson Confronts the Vietnamese People

Shortly after Kennedy's death, Secretary of Defense McNamara reported to the new president, Lyndon Johnson, on South Vietnam. McNamara said the situation was bad, and that if the United States did not act, a new Communist or neutral government would be in power in South Vietnam within three months. The government that replaced Diem was indecisive, and the NLF was gaining support in the countryside. The Secretary of Defense counseled that the United

States should keep a close watch on Southeast Asia and be prepared to act.

From December, 1963, until the Gulf of Tonkin Resolution in August, 1964, the Johnson administration supported secret military operations in South Vietnam and against the North, and at the same time was planning broader US involvement in the war. US-supported raids and attacks on the North were carried out in the spring of 1964, air strikes were made against targets in Laos, and destroyer patrols were maintained in the Gulf of Tonkin in North Vietnamese waters. The Joint Chiefs of Staff had proposed escalation of the war and extensive bombing in January, 1964. William Bundy of the State Department was preparing a scenario for US escalation in May, 1964, a scenario that would include requesting a resolution of support for administration action by Congress. Meanwhile, members of the administration were making public statements warning of the need for greater US involvement and periodically claiming that US participation in the Southeast Asian war could end within two years.

President Johnson, planning for his own campaign for election against right-wing Republican Senator Barry Goldwater, gave no public clues to the conclusions being reached by his advisors concerning the US role in Vietnam. While Johnson was preparing for brutal war in Vietnam, US liberals were supporting him as he was promoted as the "peace candidate."

The Gulf of Tonkin incident provided the immediate pretext for implementing the scenario of escalation. Two US ships were purportedly attacked by North Vietnamese boats on August 2 and 4, 1964, in the Gulf of Tonkin. As a result of the "attack" the United States sent fighter-bombers to counterattack North Vietnam. The president then brought a resolution to Congress asking for authority to do what he deemed necessary in support of the "independence and territorial integrity" of South Vietnam and Laos.

## The Gulf of Tonkin Deception

Truth is the first casualty of war, many have said, and the Gulf of Tonkin incident falls into this category. On August 2, 1964, the American destroyer USS Maddox was patrolling the Gulf of Tonkin, adjacent to the coast of North Vietnam. The US was already waging war in both North and South Vietnam. There were three small North Vietnamese torpedo boats patrolling the Gulf of Tonkin, and the

Maddox crew was ordered to fire on them if they came within 10,000 yards. When the Maddox believed the North Vietnamese boats were within that range, the Maddox opened fire. Four US fighter bombers strafed the Vietnamese torpedo boats, which returned fire. Four North Vietnamese sailors were killed, and six wounded. There were no US casualties.

Two days later, on August 4, 1964, another alleged "attack" by North Vietnamese torpedo boats reportedly took place in the Gulf of Tonkin. An internal US National Security Agency report on the incident was declassified in 2005 and it clearly stated "that no attack happened that night." Yet, both these incidents were reported to Congress and the American people as military attacks by the North Vietnamese on a US destroyer. Congress passed the Gulf of Tonkin resolution, allowing Johnson to greatly ramp up the once secret war efforts into open war.

What does seem clear is that the Johnson administration had been planning escalation in support of the South Vietnamese government in early 1964, and that the Gulf of Tonkin incident was the vehicle used to generate congressional and public support for the actions already planned. Tom Wicker reported an unnamed official as saying: "The Tonkin resolution was then brought out of Johnson's pocket to be used as the basis for legitimizing the planned expansion of the war-all that had been needed was an event to set things in motion."[7] The Gulf of Tonkin incident, then, could have been a third "staged" event in the critical junctures of US foreign-policy history: the exploitation of the Greek civil war in February, 1947, being the first and of the North Korean "invasion" of South Korea being the second. Staged or not, all three events provided opportunities for marshaling public support for escalating US imperial policies.

After the election of the "peace" candidate in November, the Johnson administration continued its planning for escalated war to defend the faltering South Vietnamese government and army. An NLF attack on a US military installation at Pleiku in February, 1965, created the rationale for beginning the bombing of North Vietnam that would continue unabated for three years. The Pentagon Papers suggest that the bombing of North Vietnam had been decided on in September, 1964, when presidential candidate Johnson was opposing Goldwater's bombing proposals. The bombing campaign, code-named Operation Rolling Thunder, was designed to force the North Vietnamese to end support for its allies in the South and to pressure them to stop fighting.

*Bombing from US planes*

## Turning Truth Upside Down

The effect of the bombing was just the opposite. North Vietnamese resolve to support the NLF increased, the Soviet Union continued material support of the North, and the efforts of the NLF in the South were increasingly successful in winning popular support. Then Johnson in 1965 ordered US troops into offensive action against the NLF and sent twenty thousand more combat troops to South Vietnam, while trying to restrict public access to information about this new commitment. In a significant speech at Johns Hopkins University, the president called for a major Marshall-Plan effort to rebuild all of Southeast Asia, and, at the same time, in a bizarre twist of logic, likened the North Vietnamese to the Nazis in the 1930s. If the United

States acted to "appease" the "communists" in Southeast Asia the way the Europeans appeased Hitler at Munich in 1938, then all of Southeast Asia would fall to this new form of "totalitarianism," according to the Johnson Administration. Johnson also raised what may be called the "puppet" theory of aggression in Southeast Asia: the NLF, still largely indigenous South Vietnamese, was a puppet of the North, which, in turn, was a puppet of the Chinese Communists and ultimately of the Soviet Union.

This theory had little foundation, since each of these organizations and countries acted independently of each other, and on some issues disagreed quite strongly. In contrast, Diem and the South Vietnamese dictators that followed him, were puppets of the US; their positions as head of a US-created South Vietnamese "government" was possible only because of US financial and military support.

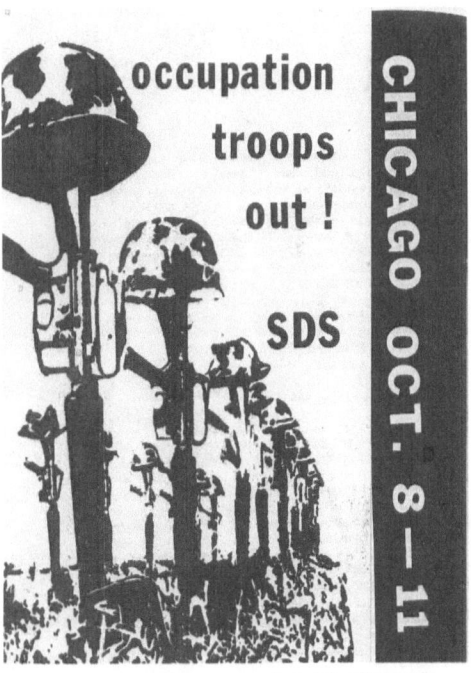

*1969 SDS Flyer*

In June, 1965, because of the deteriorating situation in the South, General Westmoreland, head of US forces in Indochina, requested forty-four battalions of troops. By July, Johnson had agreed to the Westmoreland request, and by year's end there were 184,314 US soldiers engaged in ground combat in South Vietnam. The pattern of requests for more men, coupled with promises of victory, was to continue for three years as death and destruction were unleashed on Vietnamese society. By this time opposition to the US war effort had begun to grow. A largely student-based antiwar movement began demonstrations, first on campuses and later in the streets. One of the fastest growing was Students for a Democratic Society (SDS), which organized an anti-war march in Washington DC on April 17, 1965 of 25,000 people. Other sectors of society publicly opposed the war too, including community organizations, religious groups, women's organizations, labor unions, and others. Many unions, for example, organized the national organization Labor for Peace.

*'New Age,' a labor newspaper, highlights mass march with banner 'Labor for Peace'.*

Dissent began to appear from the highest levels of society, including the government. Senator J. William Fulbright and other members of his Senate Foreign Relations Committee held public and televised hearings on the war and in the process attacked the following official administration arguments: that the United States had a moral commitment to support the South Vietnamese government, that the war was really "aggression from the North" rather than a civil-war situation, that the United States had to crush this "war of national liberation" so that Communists would learn the lesson that such wars never work, and that US prestige was at stake. Despite the growing movement against the war, US escalation continued.

In 1966 more bombings were ordered and troops sent. The latest of several generals heading the South Vietnamese government, Nguyen Cao Ky, had taken power in 1965 after several coups. His statement of admiration for Hitler was broadly disseminated in various international media outlets - but not in the US mass media, thus embarrassing those war advocates who still claimed the United States was trying to preserve democracy in Vietnam.

In 1967 the level of bombardment was again raised, from sixty to eight hundred raids per month. Johnson did not support proposals by the military to increase troop strength to 670,000, to end bombing target limits, invade Cambodia, Laos, and North Vietnam, and attack the harbor of Haiphong in the North. Even with the "constraints" placed on the military, however, large areas of South Vietnam had been declared "free fire zones," one-third to one-half of the people of Southeast Asia had become refugees, 100,000,000 pounds of herbicide were dropped on South Vietnam between 1961 and 1971, one-seventh of South Vietnam had been sprayed to destroy crops, and thirty-six percent of rice-growing swamps had been made unfit for cultivation by 1974. Between 1965 and 1971, 142 pounds of explosives per acre had been dropped on Vietnam (584 pounds per person), 118 pounds detonated per second -- all of this equivalent to 450 Hiroshima bombs. The land was being mutilated by the murderous Johnson policies, malaria was spreading, and timber and rubber industries destroyed.[8] During the Johnson years the population of Saigon

*Vietnamese women with anti-aircraft gun*

had swelled, and with wartime profiteering came incredible corruption, prostitution, and drug trafficking. Finally, by the end of 1967 more bombs had been dropped on Vietnam than had been dropped during the entire European phase of World War II.

## Tet Offensive Stuns US War-Makers

Despite the enormous firepower unleashed against the Vietnamese people, the NLF and North Vietnamese armies launched a massive assault on a number of South Vietnamese cities on January 31, 1968, during the Tet holiday. The NLF suffered large casualties but gained military control of 60 cities and large rural areas throughout South Vietnam. The US military defined their counter-attack as a victory, but key decision makers and the public knew that the war was leading to defeat. Distinguished American columnist Walter Lippmann wrote in February 1968 that the U.S. policy was crumbling and that Tet showed that military force cannot "determine the order of things on the Asian continent."[9] Three years of genocidal application of force had not reduced the spirit or resistance of the Vietnamese people.

In broad historical perspective, the Tet offensive may have provided the decisive impetus for the decline of US global power. General Westmoreland requested another 206,000 troops after Tet. Clark Clifford, a corporate lawyer who had advised Democrats on foreign policy since the Truman administration and had recently replaced McNamara as Secretary of Defense, began a quick review of US Vietnam policy. He communicated to Johnson his conclusion that the war was not winnable and therefore that Westmoreland's request should not be granted. Dean Acheson, the longtime cold warrior, told Johnson the same thing. While still wishing to pursue the war, Johnson gave in to the advice of Clifford and Acheson. The war had been so costly in men (139,801 casualties) and materiel, the value of the dollar had declined on the world market, the image of US military power had been so tarnished, and the opposition in the streets had reached such a fever pitch that key sectors of monopoly capital, which Clifford and Acheson represented, had become war critics.

## LBJ Drops Out of 1968 Race

On March 31, 1968, President Johnson announced that he was restricting the bombing to below the nineteenth parallel in the hope that the initiative would bring negotiations, and that he would not be a candidate for the presidency in 1968. The North Vietnamese responded with an offer to negotiate a full bombing halt. The Johnson administration insisted upon a reduction of North Vietnamese battle activities in the South. Despite a verbal stalemate, offensive action declined during the summer of 1968 and increased in the fall as the United States failed to respond to the decreased intensity of combat.

Finally, with the Democratic presidential candidate, Hubert Humphrey, trailing in the opinion polls, Johnson fully halted the bombing on October 31, 1968. The primary source of the U.S. defeat in Vietnam was the Vietnamese people. Domestic opposition to the brutal war played its part as well, however. The U.S. working class, not as demonstrative as students, had opposed the war more than any other group in society, according to polls; even so, worker opposition increased after Tet.

Activities of the antiwar movement also became more intense and incorporated more and more people. Growing numbers of soldiers and veterans opposed the war, and many joined Vietnam Veterans Against The War. Early anti-war groups that didn't initially have a sophisticated theory of the war, began making the connections between the war, racism and poverty. Some had gained this insight from Dr. Marin Luther King's famous anti-war speech presented at Riverside Church in New York in April, 1967.

Groups like the Students for a Democratic Society (SDS) talked of the Vietnam War as a by-product of the structure of capitalism and imperialism. These views countered earlier explanations that emphasized a misguided and overly zealous anti-Communist outlook.  As the war progressed, very large anti-war coalitions formed and organized many huge demonstrations in Washington DC, New York, San Francisco, Boston, and many other cities and towns across the country. The largest anti-war coalition was the national People's Coalition for Peace and Justice, and its predecessor, the New Mobilization Committee to End the War in Vietnam, both of which included many hundreds of organizations representing students and youth, soldiers and veterans, religious groups, women, civil rights organizations, labor, community groups, socialists and communists, and many others.

Corresponding to the antiwar sentiment among the corporate elites represented by Clifford and Acheson was a reformist electoral movement to end the war.  This was led by Senators Eugene McCarthy and later Robert Kennedy who entered presidential primaries and scored victories over President Johnson. Tensions within the society were heightened when Senator Kennedy and civil rights leader and later antiwar activist Martin Luther King were assassinated. Finally, in the summer of 1968 thousands of antiwar activists and other dissidents came to the Democratic National Convention in Chicago, where they were brutally beaten by the Chicago police. The Democrats ignored McCarthy's victories in the primaries and the massive protest against the war outside the convention and selected Johnson's vice president, Hubert Humphrey, as the presidential candidate. To a large extent, as slogans of the time ran, the war had indeed been brought home.

## Nixon's Secret Plan: Indiscriminate Bombing

During the 1968 presidential campaign, candidate Nixon declared that he had a "secret plan" to end the war in Vietnam. This secret plan had to be one in which the United States pursued victory in Southeast Asia and, at the same time, reduced the levels of US blood andresources expended on the war.  Nixon's policy during the next four years involved just such a scheme: pursuit of victory and withdrawal at the same time. The ultimate failure of this duplicitous policy is attributable to the courageous struggle of the Vietnamese and the significant resistance from the antiwar movement at home.

In June, 1969, President Nixon met with his South Vietnamese counterpart, President Nguyen Van Thieu, on Midway Island. At this meeting the policy called "Vietnamization," an application of the "Nixon Doctrine," was unveiled. The United States would withdraw all its

*Vietnam Moratorium in DC*

ground troops from South Vietnam over the next four years. This would undercut the primary reason for opposition to the war at home. The United States would substitute a massive, unrestrained bombing campaign for the withdrawn troops. Almost all the target restrictions in the South and North would be lifted. A secret bombing campaign against North Vietnamese supply routes would ensue, with bombings in neutral Cambodia as well as the continuation of secret bombing in Laos. At the meeting, Nixon and Thieu planned for the withdrawal of 85,000 of the 550,000 U.S. troops by September, 1969. This new Vietnam policy illustrated what Nixon meant by giving assistance to allies while they carried the major burden of regional conflicts. The South Vietnamese army would shed its blood while the United States provided the materiel and the air power to defeat the liberation forces.

The announcement of some of the Nixon plan, namely, the proposed troop withdrawals, did not stifle the opposition to the war in Congress or in the streets. A Vietnam Moratorium Day was held in thousands of cities, towns and rural areas in every state in the country, involving an estimated 2 million people with a full and immediate end to the war as the central demand. On November 15, 1969, over a half a million anti-war protestors converged on Washington, D.C. to protest the war. Two hundred and fifty thousand antiwar activists had a "March Against Death" in front of the Capitol and White House. During this time news of the brutal U.S. massacre of five hundred people in the village of My Lai reached the public. While this massacre was only one of many massacres and war crimes committed by the U.S., as detailed by journalist Nick Turse in his book Kill Anything That Moves: The Real American War in Vietnam, it was one of the few such massacres that received mass media coverage.

In March, 1970, the neutralist regime of Prince Sihanouk in Cambodia was overthrown by the right-wing general Lon Nol, supported by the United States. Although Sihanouk had tried desperately for several years to keep his country out of the war, the North Vietnamese did have bases in Cambodia, and the United States had been bombing and raiding areas in which the bases were thought to be located. Sihanouk's opposition to the US incursions and his cordial relationship with the Chinese was an annoyance to the United States.

## War Expands
## To Cambodia

On April 30, 1970, one month after the coup in Cambodia, Nixon announced that a force of South Vietnamese and 16,000 US troops had invaded Cambodia to destroy the Vietnamese bases. This escalation of the war into another country was defended as a vehicle to accelerate the US withdrawal. The reaction on college campuses in the United States was unprecedented. Campuses all over the country were closed down, with huge demonstrations occurring at many more. At two such campuses, Jackson State University in Mississippi and Kent State University in Ohio, student activists were shot and killed - by police authorities in the former case and by the Ohio National Guard in the latter. These shootings were seen as part of a national policy encouraged by the Nixon administration to kill or jail dissidents of all kinds under the call for "law and order." Nixon's attorney general had already instituted a policy of extermination of members of the Black Panther party in 1969, and the shootings on privileged campuses suggested an escalation of repression of dissent, even middle-class dissent.

Even members of the US Senate were outraged by the invasion of Cambodia. They passed the so-called Church-Cooper amendment, which ended funds for making war in Cambodia after July 1, 1970. The Senate also repealed the Gulf of Tonkin resolution. Sixty percent of the US public, according to opinion polls, favored withdrawal from Vietnam as well.

After the withdrawal from Cambodia of the invading army, the Nixon administration claimed that the assault had been a great success. What was not said was that the presumed North Vietnamese command headquarters, believed to be in Cambodia, was never located. The impact of the Cambodian coup and the invasion following it was criminal, since the fabric of another Indochinese society had been destroyed. By 1975, 700,000 Cambodians had died as a result of the invasion and the civil war that resulted from the coup. Two hundred and fifty thousand tons of bombs had been dropped on Cambodia. One-half of the population was homeless by 1975. By the time the forces of Pol Pot had gained control of the country, after his victory over Lon Nol in 1975, the land had been devastated. Pol Pot and the Khmer Rouge then engaged in policies that led to the deaths of more than a million people. They supported border attacks on Vietnam. Finally, in December, 1978, Vietnam sent troops into Cambodia to put an end to the murderous Pol Pot regime. The tragedies experienced by Cambodians since 1970 have to be seen as linked to the destruction of that society by US military power from 1969 to 1975.

In February, 1971, South Vietnamese troops invaded Laos to capture the Ho Chi Minh trail, the major supply route from North to South. The United States provided air support for the operation. The invasion was a military disaster, as one-half the South Vietnamese troops were killed. Morale in the South Vietnamese army declined markedly.

Elsewhere, significant moves were being taken by the Nixon administration. Along with the "stick" of repression of dissent at home (surveillance, arrests, killings, infiltration of radical groups to provoke irresponsible actions, etc.), the "carrot" was applied as well - the draft laws were changed. First, a lottery system made some young men exempt from military service, through the luck of the draw. Second, there was movement toward an all-volunteer army. Changes in the draft laws reduced the intensity of commitment among many antiwar activists. These changes were also supposed to reduce the level of dissent, which had reached dramatic proportions within the military itself. Blacks and poor whites, the largest numbers of those populating the military, were deserting, disobeying orders, refusing to

*NLF Fighters*

fight, and escaping the brutality of the battlefield through the use of drugs. Many also participated in large anti-war protests organized by the Vietnam Veterans Against the War and other groups. Protesting veterans and other anti-war activists established anti-war GI coffee houses near US military bases.

The progressive withdrawal of US troops continued as the United States supplied the South Vietnamese with new weapons, more train- ing, and supported the return of South Vietnamese officials to the villages. All of this failed. The NLF and their sympathizers contin- ued the struggle with even greater determination, while conscripted South Vietnamese soldiers were less than enthusiastic about their fate. Corruption, brutality, and repression continued to characterize the Thieu regime.

## Negotiations Pick Up

Growing numbers of people in both Vietnam and the United States were demanding an end to the war and the removal of all US troops and military. Yet, the negotiating process between the North Viet- namese and the United States, which began formally in January, 1969, continued with little result. The United States called for a cease-fire in place and a withdrawal of all "foreign" troops, while the North Vietnamese denied that they had troops in the South and refused to accept a cease-fire that would benefit the Thieu regime to the detriment of the mass of the Vietnamese people, who opposed this regime.

Kissinger, the president's national security advisor, and the North Vietnamese began secret negotiations in 1971. Nixon publicized these talks in January, 1972, to further forestall the critics of his policy. The North Vietnamese, for their part, resented this violation of secret diplomacy, and hostilities on the battlefield increased. On March 30, 1972, seven days after the United States indefinitely suspended the peace talks in Paris, the North Vietnamese and the NLF launched a new offensive. The United States responded on May 8, 1972, with massive bombing of the North and the mining of the international harbor at Haiphong, in the Democratic Republic of Vietnam, called North Vietnam by the US government and media. This dangerous escalation of the war -- Soviet supply ships docked at Haiphong -- was carried out just before Nixon was scheduled to go to Moscow.

Talks were held in Paris periodically in the summer and fall of 1972, while the bombing in North and South continued. On October 26, 1972, just before the US presidential elections, Kissinger announced that "peace is at hand" in Vietnam. Apparently Kissinger and his counterparts had reached some agreements on a cease-fire. President Thieu, however, raised many objections to the accords, and when Kissinger brought these back to Paris, the North Vietnamese countered with their own objections. Peace was not at hand, but Nixon won a major electoral victory against antiwar candidate Senator George McGovern twelve days after the Kissinger claim.

During November and December the negotiations had been brought near completion but were stalled because of the intransigence of Thieu (supported by Kissinger); then the Nixon administration began the saturation bombing of Hanoi and the rest of North Vietnam on December 18. This so-called Christmas bombing lasted until December 30. Nathan and Oliver claim this bombing was designed to force the North to sign a cease-fire and to encourage the support of a recalcitrant President Thieu from South Vietnam, who had not been adequately consulted during the negotiation process. Therefore, the barbarity of Nixon and Kissinger's decisions until the very end was based on backing a dictatorial regime that never had any support among the Vietnamese working people. "Thieu, now satisfied that the North had been seriously weakened and mollified by the US show of force, finally went along, and the negotiations were concluded on January 27, 1973."[10]

*December 22, 1970 bombing of factory in Hanoi*

## Vietnamese Liberation Forces Win

From the cease-fire of January, 1973, to the spring of 1975, the NLF and South Vietnamese armies jockeyed for military advantage. For example, within three months of the Paris accords the South Vietnamese army launched many operations against areas held by the Provisional Revolutionary Government (PRG), a broad coalition government of all those opposed to the Thieu regime and the US war. Finally, in 1975, the PRG capture of two strategic district towns initiated a fifty-five day battle that led to the final defeat of the South Vietnamese army, the creation of and clients of the United States.

The Pol Pot forces were victorious in Cambodia, followed by Communist-led forces in Laos. President Ford, who had replaced Nixon after he was forced to resign over the Watergate scandal, called for military support for the South Vietnamese army in early 1975, but Congress would not go along.

After a thirty-year struggle in Vietnam, years of civil war in Laos, and five years of war and civil war in Cambodia, the workers and peasants of Indochina were victorious against imperialism. The respite from violence was brief, however, and the horrendous impact of war on society and environment was to persist. Unfortunately, conflicts indigenous to Southeast Asia and infused by imperialism's refusal to leave the people of the area alone would involve different struggles after 1975.

The failed U.S. effort to win the imperialist war in Southeast Asia, or, as some say, the effort to postpone losing the war, had such horrendous consequences for the local population that genocide is the best label to describe the twenty-five year policy of the United States. As a result of the war, estimates range from 1.3 million to 3 million Vietnamese killed and three million wounded. Huge areas of fertile land were made waste and rubble. Three times the amount of bombs dropped in World War II were dropped on the Vietnamese.

The US suffered from the grotesque war as well: 56,000 US soldiers died during the course of the war and 303,600 were wounded. Untold millions, Vietnamese and Americans, have suffered since the war from genetic diseases brought on by Agent Orange. The cost of the war, which in no small way was reflected in poverty and misery at home, was $155 billion from 1955 to 1974.[11] The facts about this mass murder and waste of human resources would not be forgotten by progressive peoples around the world, who would work all the harder to destroy the structure of imperialism that necessitates such policies.

For the Vietnamese people, Nguyen Khac Vien suggested, the struggles for human development continued albeit in a more complex way: "After 1975 the development of history is more complex, and the historian can no longer be satisfied with any dichotomic vision which was so often put forward during the years of war: national-anti-national, communist-anti-communist, East-West, socialist-capitalist and so on. National and international issues, economic, political social, religious, cultural and ethnic questions were intertwined at different levels with discrepancies in time and complex interaction, creating an imbroglio for which no schema or model can give an exhaustive explanation."[12]

Nguyen Khac Vien was not rejecting the long and painful struggle for national liberation that the Vietnamese people had committed their lives to but rather was pointing out that the next phase of their struggle, rebuilding their Socialist country, was a project that would be as difficult, if not more so, than defeating imperialism. He recognizes there are inherent contradictions in capitalism that cause exploitation and oppression for many, and that the only solution is to build a new society based on cooperation and caring, Socialism.

## Footnotes

1. Nguyen Khac Vien, Vietnam: A Long History, The Gioi Publishers, Ha Noi, 2007, 243.

2. President Dwight Eisenhower, "Remarks at Governors' Conference, August 4, 1953, Public Papers of the Presidents, 1953, 540.

3. Marvin E Gettleman, ed., Vietnam, New York,:Fawcett, 1966.

4. Nguyen Khac Vien, 260.

5. Neil Sheehan, ed., The Pentagon Papers,, New York: Bantam, 1971, 129.

6. Nguyen Khac Vien, 271.

7. Tom Wicker, JFK and LBJ, Baltimore: Penquin, 1969, 224-225.

8. James A. Nathan and James K. Oliver, United States Foreign Policy and World Order, Boston: Little, 1976, 369-370.

9. Nguyen Khac Vien, 283.

10. James A. Nathan and James K. Oliver, 389.

11. Alexander De Conde, A History of American Foreign Policy. Volume 2. New York:Scribner's, 1978, 380.

12. Nguyen Khac Vien, 335.

# Chapter 8.  What You Can Do to Build Solidarity and Friendship with Vietnam

The US left and progressive movement has a long history of solidarity with the Vietnamese people and their revolution, stemming from our responsibility to redress our government's crimes and our internationalism.  These ties are a precious legacy of the war as we have learned from and supported each other.

Now, as Vietnam works to overcome the longstanding effects of the US war and to build socialism in a complex international reality, here are some ways we can continue to develop solidarity and friendship.

**1.  Take part in the struggle for justice for Agent Orange victims in Vietnam, in the US and throughout the world.**  Agent Orange remains the most serious consequence of the US war for millions of people. The Vietnam Agent Orange Relief & Responsibility Campaign (www.vn-agentorange.org) works throughout the US to assure that those responsible - the US government and the chemical manufacturers of Agent Orange, most prominently Dow and Monsanto, meet their responsibility to their victims.

The Campaign holds educational events, speaking tours, delegations to Vietnam and works on legislation in Congress. Congresswoman Barbara Lee will soon be introducing legislation which will provide medical, vocational and social service assistance to Agent Orange victims in Vietnam, clean up the dioxin-affected lands in Vietnam and provide medical care to Agent Orange affected children and grandchildren of US veterans and to Vietnamese Americans.

"Go to: vn-agentorange.org to sign a postcard to your representative in Congress asking them to support this legislation."

"Support the work of the Campaign and its partner group in Vietnam, the Vietnam Association for Victims of Agent Orange/dioxin, by clicking on the Paypal link on the website."

"Contact the Campaign to volunteer, request information or a speaker at your event or to arrange a visit to Vietnam to meet the victims. "

VIỆT-NAM TOÀN THẮNG !

**2. Develop relations with Vietnamese mass organizations**: sister to sister relations with the Vietnam Women's Union and worker to worker relations with the Vietnam General Confederation of Labor. The Vietnam Women's Union is a mass organization promoting the gender equality and the rights of women. 13 million members strong, with branches in every town, commune and hamlet in Vietnam, the Women's Union is engaged in every facet of women's lives from economic development and political power to ending domestic violence. The Vietnam General Confederation of Labor represents Vietnamese workers across the country and advocates for the interests of working people with the government.

Developing ties between these two mass movements and our movements will be a real step to enhancing enduring relations between our two peoples.

" Contact CCDS to find out more about the Vietnam Women's Union or the Vietnam General Confederation of Labor. "

" Ask your local women's group to consider an exchange with the Women's Union and/or your union to develop an exchange with its counterpart in Vietnam."

**3. Combat U.S. intervention in the internal affairs of the Vietnamese people.** The socialist, left and progressive movements have always upheld the principle of respect for the national independence and sovereignty of countries and peoples, especially in the face of US wars of intervention and imperialist domination. The US government has never summed up its experience in Vietnam correctly and continues to overthrow, invade and occupy countries around the world, whether the excuse is "weapons of mass destruction", or humanitarian intervention (also called human rights imperialism).

Despite its history of war crimes against the Vietnamese people, as amply documented in Nick Turse's recent book, *Kill Anything That Moves, The Real American War in Vietnam,* the US government still arrogantly reserves the right to try to lecture and sanction Vietnam for not living up to the US' "lofty" human rights standards! The Vietnamese people have demonstrated their concern for developing human rights under socialism.

" Oppose US government attempts to sanction Vietnam in Congress."

" Support young Vietnamese American organizers who are threatened by the Vietnamese rightwing for developing relations with Vietnam."

**4. Oppose the U.S. government's 50th anniversary "celebration" of their war against Vietnam.** The US Department of Defense is holding a year long program to commemorate the 50th anniversary of the war against Vietnam.  Though the program claims to "honor the veterans" it provides none of the hundreds of thousands of dollars allocated to the anniversary to provide any concrete assistance to veterans, many of whom are suffering economically. Instead, the commemoration will, "Highlight the advances in technology, science, and medicine related to the military research conducted during the Vietnam War." These so-called advances include Agent Orange, white phosphorus and the drones now being used against the peoples of South Asia.

"Contact Veterans for Peace to join their efforts to counter this revisionist history. "

"Organize an educational event or teaching in your school or community to let people know about the real history of the war, the continuing legacy in today's wars and the need to stop these wars."

# About the Authors

**Paul Krehbiel** was a Vietnam war resister, and a president of the Buffalo Draft Resistance Union. He was arrested three times for anti-war activities. As a union auto worker, he was a founder in 1970 of an anti-war workers' newspaper, *New Age*. Paul was a representative to the national People's Coalition for Peace and Justice. He later became a local union president, a chief union negotiator, and a national union newspaper editor. A member of CCDS in Los Angeles, he is author of *Shades of Justice*.

**Duncan McFarland** was an antiwar student activist at Oberlin College in Ohio in the 1960s. This led to the study of Marxism and eventual service on the CCDS National Coordinating Committee, and chair of the CCDS Peace and Solidarity Committee. He operated a China exchange program in the 1980s and is currently coordinator of the China Study Group, in Cambridge, Massachusetts. Since 9/11 Duncan has been a board member of United for Justice with Peace (Boston) and was co-organizer of two CCDS Vietnam study tours.

**Ngô Thanh Nhàn, Ph.D.** is a visiting scholar at NYU and Temple University and a Vietnamese Dàn Tranh musician. He is a board member of The Mekong Center, organizing the Cambodian and Vietnamese community in the Bronx, New York. Nhàn is a founding Co-Coordinator of the Vietnam Agent Orange Relief & Responsibility Campaign and has been active in his community since helping to found the Union of Vietnamese in the US in 1972. He was one of the organizers of the first National Progressive Viet Gathering.

**Merle E Ratner**, is a founding Co-Coordinator of the Vietnam Agent Orange Relief & Responsibility Campaign and a member of the Board of Directors of the Brecht Forum/New York Marxist School. She has been active in the anti-war, anti-imperialist and anti-racist movements all her life and was a coordinator of the Workshop on Marxist Theory and Practice in the World Today held jointly with the Ho Chi Minh National Political Academy in Hanoi in 2009. Merle works for an international labor rights organization.

**Harry Targ** has been teaching international relations, United States foreign policy, labor studies, international political economy, and United States/Caribbean relations for 46 years at Purdue University, in West Lafayette, Indiana. He has published books and articles on these subjects, the most recent book being Diary of a Heartland Radical, Changemaker, 2011, and he blogs at www.heartlandradical.blogspot.com  He has served on the National Executive Committee of the Committees of Correspondence for Democracy and Socialism.

**Tran Dac Loi** is the Vice-President of the Vietnam Peace and Development Foundation.

## FOR MORE INFORMATION

Committees of Correspondence for Democracy and Socialism: cc-ds.org

Communist Party of Vietnam: www.cpv.org.vn

Vietnam Agent Orange Relief and Responsibility Campaign: www.VN-agentorange.org

Vietnam Association for Victims of Agent Orange/Dioxin: www.vava.org.vn

Vietnam News: vietnamnews.vn

Vietnam Veterans Against the War: vvaw.org

Vietnam Women's Union: hoilhpn.org.vn

Women's Museum of Vietnam: www.womenmuseum.org.vn

Veterans for Peace: www.veteransforpeace.org

United for Peace and Justice: www.unitedforpeace.org

**PHOTO & ILLUSTRATION CREDITS:**

Paul Krehbiel: pages 2, 5, 7, 8, 9, 10, 11, 12, 14, 16, 17, 18, 20, 21, 22, 23, 25, 43, 46, 53, 55, 60, back cover

Felix Greene (from *Vietnam! Vietnam!*, published 1966): pages 33, 35, 36, 66, 68, 72, 75.

Duncan McFarland: page 58

# Online University of the Left

## Study! Teach! Organize!

We are a free and open university with all the diverse views on the left. We are inspired by Karl Marx, whose ideas are a common touchstone for many people working for change. His historical materialism, his many contributions to political economy and class analysis, all continue to serve our core values--the self-emancipation of the working class and a vision of a classless society. There are naturally many trends in Marxism that have developed over the years, and new ones are on the rise today. All of them, and other radicals and progressives who want to see this project succeed, are welcome here.

- Free political and cultural programming with hundreds of video classes

- Ideal for book store programs, book promotions & study groups

- Faculty: get 'double duty' out of your online materials by placing them here as well

- Course outlines & in-depth text archives; use for teach-ins. Just get a projector and a screen!

- Coming soon! Interactive classes in real time for a small fee.

- Speakers also available

- Your input & feedback is welcome! Use our Facebook page, too!

# http://ouleft.org

A Left Unity Project of the Committees of Correspondence for Democracy and Socialism
Http://cc-ds.org To get involved, contact: Carl Davidson at carld717@gmail.com

# The 'Lone Ranger' Period Is Over!
# We Need You to Join Us....

We're inviting you to join the **Committees of Correspondence for Democracy and Socialism**. We need you help in building a progressive majority for peace, justice and equality—and then pushing on to a new society where these will be the rule, rather than the exception. Socialism is being more widely discussed today than any time since the 1960s, and you can't take part in it fully without a socialist organization.

You can make a difference. Lend a hand in organizing with others to fight for a progressive agenda in the streets, workplaces, communities of faith and schools. It's not crowded up front, so sign up today!

Fill out and mail today.*

Yes, I'd like to join the CCDS. Enclosed is my check for:
$ _____.
I'd like a subscription to Dialogue & Initiative. Enclosed is my check for $12.50 (Non-Members, $15.00).  I know good causes need money. Here is my contribution of $_____.

Name _____
Address _____
City _____State_____ Zip _____
Phone_____
Email _____

Make check payable to"
Committees of Correspondence, and mail to:

Committees of Correspondence, 220 E. 42nd St, (Room 407)New York, NY 10017 Phone (212) 868-3733

Email: national@cc-ds.org Web: www.cc-ds.org

* The Committees of Correspondence for Democracy and Socialism (CCDS) is a national organization dedicated to the struggle for justice, equality, democracy, peace and socialism. The annual membership is $36 for individuals; $18 for unemployed, seniors, youth, and others with low income; $48 for households